Surrounded

by

REALITY

101 THINGS YOU DIDN'T KNOW ABOUT

ITHACA
N.Y.

(BUT ARE ABOUT TO FIND OUT)

MICHAEL TURBACK

FOREWORD BY SVANTE MYRICK
MAYOR OF THE CITY OF ITHACA

COPYRIGHT NOTICE

Printed in the United States of America.

NO CRYBABIES

"Either you deal with what is the reality, or you can be sure that the reality is going to deal with you."

— Alex Haley, Ithaca-born author of *Roots*

FOREWORD

Surrounded by Reality is a must read for anyone who wishes to know more about Ithaca and the colorful history that has shaped it. As those who have lived or spent time here know, Ithaca is an extraordinary city unlike any other. It is a place where diversity and community are celebrated, where education and innovation are encouraged, and where artistic talent and natural beauty abound.

The pieces of information that fill the pages of this book are as enlightening and amusing as they are random and remarkable. If you want to know how the Campbell's soup can, Tommy Hilfiger, and "Puff the Magic Dragon" are connected to Ithaca; if you want to know what "mistpouffers" are or why Ithaca was once called the "Evil City"; or if you simply want to know a little more about the City's history and ancestors, then you will want to read this book.

Surrounded by Reality teaches us and reminds us of all that Ithaca is and always has been. It serves as a preservation of the City's past and present, documenting some of the people and events that have passed through and highlighting the things that make Ithaca so truly special. I hope you enjoy reading it as much as I have.

Svante Myrick
Mayor, City of Ithaca

PREFACE

There is a popular bumper sticker in this Upstate New York town that reads, "Ithaca: 10 Square Miles Surrounded by Reality." The sentiment surely has something to do with the compelling history, eccentric characters, and quirky charm of this intellectually advantaged, culturally progressive, geographically isolated place. After you've browsed through this little book, you will better understand the bumper sticker's message — Ithaca is almost too good to be true.

Sure, we live here, but how much do we really know about Ithaca? What is Annie Oakley's connection to Ithaca? Who was the cub reporter for the *Ithaca Journal* who ended up building a media empire? Where are Ithaca's two spruce trees originally planted by Teddy Roosevelt? Why is Volvo the city's vehicle of choice? How did Ezra Cornell make his fortune? What in the world was Harry Houdini doing here! In *Surrounded by Reality*, readers learn the answers to these intriguing questions and much, much more.

Fascinating tidbits and trivia in purposely random sequence (with generous cross-references) create a ready-to-explore trail of knowledge about Ithaca and its environs, informing and entertaining, correcting myths and misconceptions, mostly revealing an unexpected treasure trove that brings a culture and a place into sharp focus.

CENTRALLY ISOLATED

When President Franklin Roosevelt appointed Frances Perkins the Secretary of the Department of Labor in 1933, she became the very first woman to hold a cabinet position. After moving to Ithaca to teach at Cornell's ILR school, Perkins called Ithaca "the most isolated place on the Eastern Seaboard."

With the opening of the Erie Canal and its connection to Cayuga Lake, it was expected that Ithaca would become the shipping center for grain, coal and lumber from a wide surrounding area, but with the extension of a canal from the southern end of Seneca Lake to the Susquehanna River, there came a falling off in trade. With the completion of the Ithaca and Owego Railway, it was a good bet that Ithaca would become a major commercial route, but with the Erie line to the south, and New York Central to the north, Ithaca was left stranded midway between two trunk systems. The geography of the city has always prevented Ithaca from becoming a major transportation artery.

Today, Ithaca lies at over a half hour's drive from any interstate highway, and all car trips to Ithaca involve at least some driving on two-lane state rural highways.

# ROCKET'S RED GLARE

Americans have set off fireworks to commemorate Independence Day ever since 1776, but after many over-the-top celebrations in the 1880s (once including a high-wire act on State Street), Ithaca's observances of the holiday were generally modest affairs – at least until 1948. When the local Chamber of Commerce suggested a fireworks display, donations totaling $1,000 were raised from downtown merchants, and Cornell offered the football stadium for public viewing.

The venue is now Stewart Park (see **Stewart's Park**, page 33), and American Fireworks Manufacturing, a family-run firm based in Utica, now produces a 30-minute extravaganza at a cost of $1,000 a minute (a price break for holding the show a day or two earlier than the 4th). It takes a crew of 12 pyrotechnicians and 2500 shells – cardboard balls as wide as 8-inches in diameter, filled with gun powder and chemicals. Computers remotely ignite the fireworks with an electric match that makes contact with a gun powder fuse. The gun powder, called "black powder," launches each shell as high as 800 feet in the sky.

Although some cities underwrite the cost of fireworks displays, the Ithaca event continues to rely entirely on donations. Money dropped into barrels at the entrance in one year funds the fireworks for the following year.

Sanctuary City

On October 1, 2008, the City of Ithaca declared itself a "Community of Sanctuary," aimed at allowing peaceful protests of illegal wars in the city. The City Council voted unanimously to pass the resolution to protect the right of city residents "to support lawfully and proactively military personnel and veterans who are organizing to stop the wars in and occupations of Iraq and Afghanistan and all future violations of the United Nations Nuremberg Charters."

The resolution was a reminder of Ithaca's history in an earlier sanctuary movement, the anti-slavery struggle of the 19th century, known as "the Underground Railroad." A group of abolitionists sheltered freedom seekers at St. James African Methodist Episcopal Zion Church on Cleveland Avenue, an important transfer point for fugitive slaves en route to Canada.

Among the escaped slaves who decided to stay in Ithaca was Aunt Elsie Brooks who lived out her years in a home near the church. In 1848, Frederick Douglass, one of the foremost leaders of the abolitionist movement, addressed a church-sponsored anti-slavery rally at St. James.

"ITHACA IS GORGES"

Howard Cogan was born in Philadelphia in 1929, the son of a shoe salesman. When he was six, his family moved to Ithaca where his father became the shoe buyer for Rothschild's Department Store. After graduating from Cornell in 1950, he began a lifelong career in advertising and promotion. In 1978, at the age of 49, Cogan returned to Cornell and earned a Master's degree in communications, graduating with his son, Michael as the first parent-child simultaneous graduates in the university's history.

For the following two decades, Cogan maintained his local advertising agency while teaching advertising and public relations at Ithaca College. His slogan, "Ithaca is Gorges," drawn with a waterfall replacing the letter "I," began as an inside joke about the waterfalls and gorges that carve up the city's landscape. Cogan never copyrighted the phrase, and Abdul Razak Sheikh, owner of T-Shirt Expressions on the Ithaca Commons, was the first to reproduce the original design on t-shirts in 1983.

The t-shirt has spawned a variation that describes the city's typical weather: "Ithaca is Cold."

HELL ON WHEELS

W. T. Pritchard on South Cayuga Street is one of the oldest family-owned and operated automobile and truck dealerships in North America. James G. Pritchard arrived in Ithaca from England in the late 1800s as a craftsman specializing in carriages, buggies, sleighs and wagons. He opened a manufacturing facility and sales office in Ithaca, then in 1910 began selling "horseless carriages,"or as many called them, "devilish contraptions."

The Dodge franchise was acquired in 1915, less than 12 months after Horace and John Dodge's first automobile came off the assembly line at Hamtramck, Michigan. (The Dodge brothers had worked for Henry Ford for 12 years, designing and building most of the parts for Ford, and decided it was time to build their own vehicles). James' son William moved the dealership to Cayuga Street in 1921.

In May, 2009, Chrysler announced that Pritchard was on the list of 789 dealers to be eliminated from the company's network as part its bankruptcy restructuring.

By 2011, Pritchard had become one of the first dealerships in New York to offer a plug-in vehicle, the Wheego Electric Car.

YOU'RE WELCOME,
ANDY WARHOL

John T. Dorrance, a gifted chemist with degrees from MIT and Göttingen University, Germany, developed a commercially viable method for condensing soup, eliminating much of the water without reducing the flavor or nutritional value. Within five years, his employer, the Campbell Soup Company, was selling more than 15 million cans of soup annually.

On Thanksgiving Day, 1897, Campbell's comptroller, Herberton L. Williams, a spectator at the annual Cornell-Penn football game, was so impressed by the bright colors of Cornell's red and white uniforms, he suggested that the company replace the soup label's original black and orange design. Williams' enthusiasm was formidable enough to convince management at Campbell's to adopt the Cornell color scheme, a design that endures on the classic line of soups to this day.

Pop artist Andy Warhol was fascinated by iconic American products, none more than the Campbell's soup can. His depiction of the red and white can was one of Warhol's most popular works; the original on display in the Museum of Modern Art.

CLIFFHANGERS

When brothers Theo and Leo Wharton arrived in Ithaca to film a Cornell football game for the Essanay Company, they realized they had found the ideal setting for the daring stunts and action sequences that attracted audiences to movies of the day. In April of 1914, they built a movie studio, including indoor and outdoor stages, on lakefront property (see **Stewart's Park**, page 33) where they produced some of the most popular films of the silent era.

The term "cliffhanger" comes from the weekly episodes in which a heroine would end up hanging over a cliff as a villain waited for her to plummet to her death. Theater audiences would have to return the following week to find out how the heroine would escape. The most popular Wharton serials were *The Exploits of Elaine*, starring Pearl White, and *Patria*, starring Irene Castle (see **Exploits of Irene**, page 97), both female protagonists, variously chased, rescued and wooed. Other early movie stars who worked in Ithaca include Lionel Barrymore, Francis X. Bushman, Beverly Bayne, Warner Oland (later gaining fame as "Charlie Chan") and Oliver Hardy (before teaming with Stan Laurel). Unfortunately for Ithaca, the movie-making industry left town and headed for Hollywood in 1920.

SURPLUS WEALTH

He was born in Westchester County, New York, the son of a potter, and a first cousin, five times removed, of Benjamin Franklin. Ezra Cornell traveled extensively as a carpenter throughout New York State and upon first setting eyes on Ithaca, decided to make it his home. After a number of failed ventures, he became involved in the experimental telegraph line of Samuel Morse and devised a special plow that would dig a ditch, lay pipe with a strand of wire, and cover it back up as it went. (In 1844, Cornell connected the first telegraph line between the U.S. Capitol building and the railroad station in Baltimore). By taking his pay in stock, he became the largest stockholder in the Western Union Company.

In 1857, at the age of fifty, he retired from Western Union, determined to use his surplus wealth to establish a university in his beloved Ithaca. He donated 300 acres of farmland, supervised construction of the first buildings, purchased equipment, books, and collections. On October 7, 1868, Inauguration Day, 412 students, the largest entering class admitted to any American college up to that time, arrived in Ithaca. Ezra gave a brief address, concluding with the University's adopted motto: "Finally, I trust we have laid the foundation of a University—an institution where any person can find instruction in any study."

DIFFERENT STROKES

During the late 1800s, college rowing was the era's most popular sport, and huge crowds attended the important races. The Cornell crew was coached by Charles "Pop" Courtney, who was raised in Union Springs (a small town at the north end of Cayuga Lake noted for racing yachts), and who many considered "the greatest training master of oarsmen in the world."

There would never be a race more important for the Big Red than the 1897 Intercollegiate Rowing Association (IRA) race at Poughkeepsie. Until then, both Harvard and Yale refused to race Cornell, snubbed, it was surmised, since losing to the relatively young school would be unthinkable. Cornell's win at Poughkeepsie not only established the school as a rowing power, but also proved that the "American stroke" (a long stride with little back motion) developed by Coach Courtney was superior to the "English stroke" used by both Harvard and Yale.

In a cherished Ithaca tradition, spectators watched crew races from the banks of the lake or from craft anchored near the finish line, and from an open-air observation train along East Shore Drive. The last observation train ran in 1936.

THE CHERRY ON TOP

In 1892, the soda fountain menu at Platt & Colt Pharmacy on State Street offered a dish of ice cream for a nickel, and local Unitarian minister John M. Scott often stopped in after Sunday services for a plain scoop of vanilla. One visit in particular proved memorable. "On a whim," proprietor Chester C. Platt dipped Reverend Scott's ice cream into a champagne saucer, poured cherry syrup over the top, and dressed it with a candied cherry. As the two men pondered over what to call the new concoction, Scott proposed that it be named after the day on which it was invented.

Although several cities challenge Ithaca's claim as birthplace of the sundae, an *Ithaca Journal* advertisement for Platt & Colt dated May 28, 1892, provides irrefutable evidence. The ad promotes the fountain's "Sunday" as "a new ten-cent specialty." Before long, the novel dish attracted an enthusiastic student trade, and as Cornellians returned to hometowns around the country, they spread the news to their own local fountains. By the turn-of-the-century (and with a change in spelling that distinguished the dessert from the Sabbath), ice cream sundaes were being served across America.

INSPIRED BY THE CLASSICS

New York Surveyor-General Simeon DeWitt (see **Ithaca's Founding Father**, page 47) is often given credit for providing ancient Greek and Roman names to the twenty-eight central Military Tract townships that his office mapped after the Revolutionary War. In fact, it was Irish-born Robert Harpur, the Deputy Secretary of State and Secretary of the Land Board in the infant New York State government who drew on his background as a University of Glascow-educated classical scholar to suggest names, as request by Dewitt, "that were neither English nor Indian."

The names he came up with were: Aurelius, Brutus, Camillus, Cato, Cicero, Cincinnatus, Dryden, Fabius, Galen, Hannibal, Hector, Homer, Junius, Locke, Lysander, Manlius, Marcellus, Milton, Ovid, Pompey, Romulus, Scipio, Sempronius, Solon, Sterling, Tully, Virgil, and Ulysses. Later, after acquiring a portion of the Ulysses tract at the southern end of Caygua Lake in 1804, DeWitt called the new town Ithaca, after the island home of Ulysses in Greek mythology. Harpursville in Broome County, as well as Harpur College (now Binghamton University) was named for Robert Harpur.

Grateful Eight

Built in 1827 by local carpenter Henry Balcom, the Eight-Square Schoolhouse on Upper Hanshaw Road (1/4 mile east of the Tompkins County Regional Airport) is the earliest school still existing in Tompkins County, and the only surviving brick octagonal schoolhouse in New York State. Balcom was among early Americans inspired by the octagonal structures of the ancient Greeks and Romans. Thomas Jefferson followed their example by designing an octagonal house in Bedford County, Virginia, and George Washington's Mount Vernon has its own octagonal schoolhouse.

The octagon shape was thought to provide a better learning environment because the teacher could be placed in a prominent position within the space. An octagon provided more square feet of inside space than either a rectangle or a square. And the interior was brighter, as the sun streamed through windows on eight sides instead of only four. The building's brick walls retained heat during the cold months and helped keep it cool in the in the warm weather. The building is on the National Register of Historic Places.

RHINOCEROS DROWNS IN BEEBE LAKE

Born and raised in Ithaca, where his father was a professor at Cornell, Hugh Troy enlivened the university campus from 1922 to 1927 with non-stop practical jokes. Troy imprinted a set of rhinoceros tracks in the snow, stopping at the edge of the ice on Beebe Lake, the source of campus drinking water. The next day, after a professor of zoology confirmed the tracks as being made by a rhino, people stopped drinking water while the lake was dredged for "the animal."

Troy once swiped a JESUS SAVES sign and planted it in front of the Ithaca Savings Bank. When summoned before a faculty committee for a scandal sheet that earned him a reputation as the "Einstein of Pranksters," he pinned mistletoe to the seat of his pants, then flipped up his coattails as he left the room.

After graduating from Cornell, Troy left for New York City, where he became a successful mural painter and book illustrator. One of his jokes can still be seen on the giant globe he painted in the lobby of the Daily News Building in New York. All the cities on it are national capitals, except one: Ithaca. (Troy spent his later years working for the C.I.A.).

DISNEYLAND OF GROCERY STORES

Founded in 1916 by brothers John and Walter Wegman as the Rochester Fruit and Vegetable Company, Wegmans Food Markets pioneered such grocery innovations as refrigerated display windows, vaporized spray systems for vegetables and fruits, and barcode scanners. The family-run company expanded outside the Rochester area for the first time with a store in Syracuse in 1968, then in 1977 with a store in Buffalo.

Wegmans opened an 82,000-square-foot store in Ithaca on February 28, 1988, the 38th store in the chain, and after nine years, it was torn down and replaced with a 123,000-square-foot megastore, staffed with over 500 full and part-time employees. Ithaca native Julie Jordan, of Cabbagetown Café fame, developed the Ithaca store's vegetarian hot bar, and the "Wings of Life" salad bar is straight off the menu of her former Collegetown restaurant. First in the chain to carry an organic produce line, the Ithaca store buys directly from over 20 local growers during the summer months (posting signs above the foods listing names of the farms and locations).

In 2009, Wegmans was named the best supermarket chain in America by *Consumer Reports* and consistently ranks among *Fortune's* "100 Best Companies to Work For."

ANNIE GET YOUR GUN

The original Ithaca Gun Company factory was established in 1883, located in the Fall Creek neighborhood on a slope still known as Gun Hill, where a nearby waterfall supplied the main source of energy for the plant. Led by master gunsmith William Henry Baker, the company advertised its shotguns and rifles as "the strongest, simplest, and best American guns manufactured." Ithaca field guns were lightweight, but rugged and simple, and famous for their fast lock-time. Prominent figures such as Teddy Roosevelt, John Philip Sousa, George Marshall, and Dwight Eisenhower were known to favor Ithaca firearms.

But Ithaca guns gained legendary status in the hands of Annie Oakley, the sharpshooting superstar of Buffalo Bill's Wild West Show. Using a 12-gauge double-barreled field gun, Oakley could split a playing card edge-on and put five or six more holes in it before it touched the ground.

Before the company's demise, Ithaca shotguns were used by both Los Angeles and New York Police Departments, and sold to the Royal Thai Army in the early 1980s to arm farmers against communist infiltrators.

BEST BOOK EVER WRITTEN?

Vladimir Nabokov's novel *Lolita* has been called both "the filthiest book ever written" and "the best book ever written." Nabokov came to Ithaca in 1948 to teach Russian Literature at Cornell at the urging of Morris Bishop, Professor of Romance Literature and University Historian. After just a few months in a small apartment at 957 East State Street, Nabokov and his family moved into more comfortable quarters at 802 East Seneca Street. It was primarily at these two homes where he wrote *Lolita*. In fact, in 1950 while living at the Seneca Street residence, the volatile author attempted to burn a rough draft of the literary masterpiece in the house's incinerator, prevented only by the pleading of his wife Vera.

According to Nabokov's biographer, Brian Boyd, to develop an ear for his title character's speech pattern "he would travel on buses around Ithaca and record phrases, in a little notebook, from young girls that he heard coming back from school." Within a year after the debut of *Lolita* in America in 1958, Nabokov left Cornell. He had earned enough money from the book that he could afford to stop teaching and write full-time, and he spent the rest of his life in Montreux, Switzerland. *Lolita* has sold over 50 million copies.

PUFF'S DADDY

One night in 1959, Cornell physics major Leonard "Lenny" Lipton stopped by the library on his way to meet his friend, Lenny Edelstein, for dinner. Lipton leafed through a book of poems by Ogden Nash, and read one titled, *The Tale of Custard the Dragon*. When Lipton arrived at his friend's apartment, no one was home, so he let himself in. While he waited for Edelstein, Lipton reflected on his carefree childhood days and loss of innocence as he grew into adulthood. Inspired by Nash's poetry, Lipton sat at Edelstein's roommate's typewriter for three minutes and dashed off a poem he called "Puff, the Magic Dragon."

When the roommate came home, he found the poem in the typewriter. That roommate just happened to be Peter Yarrow, president of the Cornell Folk Music Club, who eventually put music with the words. Yarrow began performing the song with Peter, Paul and Mary at live concerts. "Puff, the Magic Dragon" was recorded by the group in 1963 and is so well-known that it has become an American musical classic.

Lipton became an expert in 3-D technology, a filmmaker, and author of *Independent Filmmaking*, the standard text on the subject.

"NOBLE SAVAGES"

The word "Coreorgonel" translates to "where we keep the pipe of peace," the name for an area near Cayuga Lake inlet, just west of Buttermilk Falls, where Native Americans of the Tutelo tribe settled in 1753, having been driven from their lands further south by white settlers. Twenty-six years later, under the orders of George Washington, Major General John Sullivan's army burned and razed much of Coreorgonel, in a scorched earth campaign against the "noble savages" who had sided with the British in the Revolutionary War.

The Tutelos managed to flee before Sullivan's army arrived on September 24, 1779. Most trekked 120 miles to Fort Niagara, seeking refuge at the British stronghold, while many starved or froze to death in the harsh early winter conditions. Remaining Tutelos eventually scattered to Canada, Oklahoma, and Wisconsin, and the last known Tutelo speaker died in 1898.

Tutelo Park, just off Bostwick Road, commemorates Ithaca's original inhabitants with wooded nature trails and native wildflower plantings. It has the county's largest shagbark hickory and black oak trees, and is home to many species of wild birds.

HOLLYWOOD ENDING

In 1914, actress Mary Pickford attained motion picture stardom with her performance in the film adaptation of the novel, *Tess of the Storm Country*. The classic melodrama allowed Ms. Pickford to display her acting chops, a role she would reprise eight years later in a 1922 adaptation by noted silent film director John S. Robertson. It would be considered the finest performance in the career of "America's Sweetheart."

Grace Miller White, the author of *Tess*, was born and lived her whole life in Ithaca. She began her writing career novelizing plays, before turning her hand to novels in 1909, the year she published *Tess*, the first of five *Storm Country* novels that centered on Cayuga Lake, Ithaca, and "the rich or poor, the righteous or lawless people who lived here."

Besides the two Pickford films, *Tess of the Storm Country* was adapted for the big screen in 1932 (starring Janet Gaynor) and in 1960 (starring Diane Baker). While Pickford's versions were shot in California, a sequel, *The Secret of Storm Country*, was filmed in Ithaca, starring another popular actress, Norma Talmadge, as Tess Skinner.

GRANDE DAME OF ITHACA

Downtown Ithaca was once home to 17 theatres, including the Lyceum, the Crescent, and the Strand, but none so grand as the State Theatre, transformed by the Berinsteins, a family of entertainment professionals, from an auto garage into a "cinema palace and vaudeville hall." They hired Pittsburgh architect Victor A. Rigaumont to design a showplace in "Collegiate Gothic," displaying Oxford College shields along the proscenium arch with Cornell and other Ivy League schools represented at the sides. Elements included leaded and stained glass panels, an arched midnight-blue ceiling illuminated with twinkling stars, and a moving cloud machine.

Ithaca's State Theatre first opened its doors on December 6, 1928, for a 6 o'clock showing of *Show Girl*, a talkie starring Alice White as Dixie Dugan, a Brooklyn-born dancer who conquers Broadway and Hollywood. The organist was Harry Springer and admission was 50 cents for adults, 30 cents for kids. While the State Theatre flourished as a premier entertainment venue for almost seven decades, the building was condemned in 1997, eventually rescued from demolition by the non-profit Historic Ithaca organization (see **Saved from the Wrecking Ball**, page 82). An official reopening was held December 5, 2001.

CITIZEN HEARST

In *Citizen Kane*, considered by many to be the greatest motion picture of all time, Charles Foster Kane, the title character played by Orson Welles, was expelled from a number of Ivy League colleges, including Cornell. But that's not the film's only connection to Ithaca. It's no secret that Welles and co-writer Herman Mankiewicz used newspaper tycoon William Randolph Hearst as a model for the obsessive Charles Foster Kane.

In real life, Hearst's mistress was actress Marion Davies, rumored to be the inspiration for the Susan Alexander character in *Kane*. Davies' career inspired Hearst to dabble in the movie business, and he provided financial backing for a number of films, including *Beatrice Fairfax*, produced in 1916 by the Wharton Brothers studio (see **Cliffhangers**, page 7), shot mostly in Ithaca. The fifteen-episode serial was the story of a columnist for the Hearst newspapers (Beatrice), played by Grace Darling. Davies makes a brief appearance (other guest stars included Mae Hopkins and Olive Thomas), and the first episode includes a cameo by William Randolph Hearst as himself.

ROCK OF AGES

In 1958, Ithaca native Bobby Comstock put together a band called Bobby & The Counts, performing rock versions of country and rhythm & blues tunes in the auditorium of Ithaca's Boynton Junior High School. The group included Comstock, Fred and Chuck Ciaschi, Gus Eframson, and Dale Sherwood.

Bobby & The Counts hit the big time with a remake of an old Patti Page song 'Tennessee Waltz,' performed on Dick Clark's *Saturday Night Beachnut Show* on December 12, 1959, followed by an appearance on *American Bandstand* on February 23, 1960 with the release of "Jambalaya." Over 20 years, Bobby's band provided backup instrumentation for such stars as Chuck Berry, Bo Diddley, Gene Pitney, Johnny Tillotson, Bobby Vee, Shirley Ellis, Sonny and Cher, Paul Revere and the Raiders, The Crystals, The Orlons, Dick and Dee Dee, Paul and Paula, The Angels, Lou Christie, The Dovells, Barbara Lewis, The Tymes, Bobby Lewis, The Shirelles, The Coasters, Bobby Vinton, Five Satins, Gary U.S. Bonds, Ruby and the Romantics, Bob B. Soxx and the Blue Jeans, and "Big Dee" Irwin.

ITHACA'S CINEMATOGRAPHER

In the film industry, the cinematographer is responsible for the technical aspects of the images (lighting, lens choices, composition, exposure, filtration, film selection), working closely with the director to ensure that the artistic aesthetics support the director's vision. Ray June, a native Ithacan and graduate of Cornell, began his career at Wharton Studios (see **Cliffhangers**, page 7) and became one of America's finest cinematographers.

After serving as a Signal Corps cameraman during World War I, he journeyed to Hollywood. With his experience working without frills, he was a natural for the low budget "quickies" of the 1920s. His camerawork on *Horse Feathers* (1932) is as hilariously haphazard as the Marx Brothers themselves. Other notable films include *I Cover the Waterfront*, *Barbary Coast*, *Treasure Island*, *China Seas*, and *Wife Versus Secretary*.

His work at MGM helped develop what became known as "the MGM look" – a rich, elegant, glossy veneer that set the studio's product apart from every other. In 1957, he was nominated for an Academy Award for *Funny Face* with Fred Astaire and Audrey Hepburn.

THE MUSEUM THAT
FLOOR WAX BUILT

In 1886 Samuel Curtis Johnson formulated a product to care for parquet floors, and 87 years later his grandson, Herbert Fisk Johnson, Jr., became the primary benefactor of the art museum perched atop a 1,000-foot slope on the northwest corner of the Arts Quad of the Cornell campus. Some say its massive reinforced concrete form suggests a sewing machine, a piano, or a giraffe, but its design (by architect I.M. Pei) is not the only source of controversy.

The museum was built on the very spot where Ezra Cornell (see **Surplus Wealth**, page 8) stood when he announced his intention to found the university, in opposition to the wishes of Andrew Dickson White, the university's co-founder and first president, who insisted that no building be constructed on this hallowed ground. Pei called his desire to build on the site "an obsession."

One element of the original design, abandoned as impractical, was an underground Asian art gallery which would have included windows breaching the Southern face of Fall Creek Gorge.

"STORM COUNTRY"

While the title may have been bestowed by a local novelist (see **Hollywood Ending**, page 19), it is true that Ithaca lies in the median storm track of the west wind belt. As a result, practically every weather disturbance that crosses the United States from the west is felt here. Overcast skies are common, and only Seattle, Washington, has fewer "sunshine days" per year than Ithaca.

Temperatures have an extraordinary range, from 102 degrees to 20 degrees below zero Fahrenheit. On average, Ithaca's warmest month is July, with an average of 71 degrees; January is coldest, with an average of 24 degrees. September is Ithaca's rainiest month, with an average of 4.21 inches. Average annual precipitation measures 35.4 inches of rain; 67.3 inches of snow.

The phenomenon of mixed precipitation (rain, wind, and snow), common in the late fall and early spring, is called "Ithacation" by the locals. Only in Ithaca can you experience all the seasons in a single day. About the erratic changes from one season to the next, it is often said, "If you don't like the weather in Ithaca, just wait a few minutes."

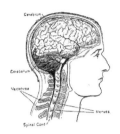

BRAIN DEPOSITORY

In 1889, Dr. Burt Green Wilder, former Civil War surgeon and founder of Cornell's Anatomy Department, established a human brain collection at the university. Wilder wanted to learn if differences in size, shape, chemistry, or weight could account for certain behaviors or personality types, including criminals and the mentally ill. Wilder's most interesting brain was that of Edward Rulloff, a self-taught genius, well-versed in history, philosophy, mineralogy, biology, and philology, the study of language formation – he spoke 28 languages and dialects.

But Rulloff possessed a dark side. Between 1845 and his hanging in 1871, Rulloff was accused of a string of burglaries and robberies, as well as several murders, including the poisoning of his sister-in-law and niece, and the beating deaths of his wife and daughter, whom he allegedly disposed of in Cayuga Lake. Upon post-mortem examination, Dr. Wilder declared Rulloff's brain the largest on record.

At its peak, the collection had some 600 specimens. Eventually many were tossed out, but Rulloff's brain remains part of the reduced collection to this day, displayed on the second floor of Uris Hall.

BIRDMAN OF ITHACA

A native Ithacan and arguably one of the most renown and influential bird artists of the 20th Century, Louis Agassiz Fuertes gave the Sapsucker Woods Sanctuary its name after his local discovery of the first Yellow-Bellied Sapsucker nest found in the Cayuga Lake basin. Born on February 7, 1874, he was named after Louis Agassiz, a Harvard professor and naturalist. Growing up in Ithaca, young Louis displayed an interest in sketching birds, and at age 14, he painted his first bird – a male Red Crossbill. Fuertes christened Sapsucker Woods one morning in June 1909 when he discovered the nest of a Yellow-Bellied Sapsucker, the first-ever breeding recorded in the Cayuga Lake basin.

From 1923 to 1927 he was a lecturer in ornithology at Cornell. The bird sanctuary at Stewart Park was named for Fuertes following his untimely death on August 22, 1927. He was killed when his car was struck by a southbound Delaware-Hudson express train at Potter's Crossing in the Broome County town of Unadilla. He left a collection of over a thousand field sketches and studio watercolors depicting more than 400 different varieties of birds.

 # MYSTERY BOOMS

The occasional sounds of cannon or sonic booms heard in Ithaca and around Cayuga Lake are known as "mistpouffers." The phantom thunder is heard on days when there are no storms in the vicinity that could produce thunder and no other obvious source. Sometimes it is accompanied by a rumble that can be felt strongly enough to rattle plates and hanging pictures; other times no vibration is felt. The lake seems to be speaking to the surrounding hills, which send back the echoes of its voice in reply.

Native Indians believed the booms were the sound of the Great Spirit continuing his work of shaping the earth. Modern theory suggests the noise is a sonic shock wave caused by expansion of air focused anomalously as it travels through the upper atmosphere. The phenomenon is also known to occur near the banks of the river Ganges in India, as well as areas of the North Sea, Japan and Italy.

Another term for mistpouffers is "Seneca Guns," originating in Seneca, Georgia, during the Civil War when the rumble of artillery fire could be felt for a distance of up to five miles from the battlefield.

WINGS OVER ITHACA

English expatriate aviators William and Oliver Thomas started building airplanes in Ithaca in 1914, at what is still known as the "Aeroplane Factory" near Cayuga Inlet. Some parts were made at the Morse Chain (now Emerson Transmission) factory on South Hill, when the Thomas Brothers Company merged with Morse Chain to become Thomas-Morse. Shortly after America's entrance into World War I, a production order was placed for 500 single-seat, open-cockpit biplanes.

Dubbed "Tommy" by the company's ace test pilot, Tex Marshall, the S-4 Scout was used as an advanced trainer to develop war-fighting skills against the German Luftwaffe. When equipped as a gunnery trainer, the Tommy was fitted with a Marlin .30-caliber aircraft machine gun mounted on the right side of the fuselage. The gun was synchronized to fire through the propeller arc, and ammunition was carried in a compartment built integrally with the fuel tank. When the war ended, Tommies were sold as surplus to civilian flying schools and private pilots. Some were still being used in the mid-1930s for World War I aviation movies filmed in Hollywood.

VIOLIN PRACTICE

Leaving his Danby home as a young man for violin studies abroad, William Grant Egbert confided his desire to establish a conservatory in nearby Ithaca so that others wouldn't have to travel so far from home to study music. When he returned from lessons in Berlin, Germany, he assembled eight faculty members and two lecturers. On September 19, 1892, with an enrollment of 125 students, the Ithaca Conservatory of Music began lessons in four rented rooms in a house on East Seneca Street. Instruction was given in violin (headed by Egbert himself), voice (taught by his wife, Gertrude Walker Egbert), keyboard and string instruments, history, biography, and modern fencing.

By 1897, studies in elocution, dance, physical education, speech correction, radio, business, and the liberal arts were added to the curriculum. In 1910, the school had secured permanent quarters with the purchase of Judge Douglass Boardman's handsome Italianate townhouse at 120 East Buffalo Street, adjoining DeWitt Park.

In 1931, Egbert's conservatory was chartered as Ithaca College, and by 1968, all academic departments had moved to the South Hill campus.

AGITATING
A BAG OF WIND

In 1874, Cornell president Andrew D. White would not allow Cornellians to travel to Cleveland for a football game against the University of Michigan, explaining "I refuse to let 40 of our boys travel 400 miles merely to agitate a bag of wind."

By 1915, however, football had become part of Ithaca culture with the opening of Schoellkopf Field. That year Charley Barrett scored a first-quarter touchdown to lead Cornell to a 10-0 victory over Harvard in a game of unbeatens. The Big Red handed the Crimson its first loss in four years and was declared national champion, the first of five national titles for Cornell. The 1939 team posted a 8-0 record, defeating Syracuse, Princeton, Penn State, Columbia, Colgate, Dartmouth, Penn, and Big Ten champion Ohio State. Cornell overcame a 14-0 deficit in the first quarter to beat the powerful Buckeyes 23-14 in Columbus. The rumor of an invitation to the Rose Bowl was quickly quelled by the administration which did not wish to further distract the players from their studies.

PLANET ITHACA

After receiving a Doctorate in astronomy from the University of Chicago, Carl Sagan joined the Harvard College astronomy faculty as Assistant Professor. Denied tenure at Harvard, Sagan moved to Cornell University in 1968, serving as David Duncan Professor of Astronomy and Director of the Laboratory for Planetary Studies until his death in 1996. Among the most important thinkers of the 20th Century, Sagan popularized astronomy, astrophysics and science, most notably in the award-winning PBS series *Cosmos: A Personal Voyage*, seen by 600 million viewers in over 60 countries. He became familiar to TV viewers from 26 appearances on *The Tonight Show* with Johnny Carson. He advised NASA during its most adventurous years and influenced a generation of planetary scientists.

Sagan lived in one of Ithaca's most interesting houses, the former home of Cornell's Sphinx Head Society, modeled on an Egyptian temple and perched on the edge of Fall Creek gorge. A year after his death, the Sciencenter (see **The Little Science Project That Grew**, page 91) created the Sagan Planet Walk, a scale model of the solar system that winds its way through the city.

STEWART'S PARK

Originally Military Tract Lot No. 88, granted to Cavalry Captain Andrew Moody of the Revolutionary Army, the land surrounding the southern tip of Cayuga Lake was sold to James Renwick in 1790 and remained in that family, undeveloped, for 104 years. In 1894 the Cayuga Lake Electric Railway Company constructed a trolley line to the lake and developed Renwick Park, a private swimming and amusement park containing a zoo, a merry-go-round, and a miniature train that supposedly ran on the world's smallest steam engine.

By 1915, with not enough patrons willing to pay for admittance, the venture was losing money. Trolley access was discontinued and the park was shut down. The land was leased to the Wharton brothers during Ithaca's brief heyday as a silent film production center (see **Cliffhangers**, page 7), from 1915 to 1919. During his inauguration speech in 1920, Mayor Edwin C. Stewart declared it a "travesty" that Ithacans couldn't enjoy the lake without trespassing on private property. He convinced the city to purchase the lake shore property and open it to the public. Mayor Stewart died before the official opening of the park on the Fourth of July in 1921, christened in his honor.

 # LONGEST HOME RUN

Cornell's baseball team plays on David F. Hoy Field, named for university registrar and baseball faculty advisor, the "Davy" of the university fight song, "Give My Regards to Davy" (see **Best Regards**, page 74).

The first baseball game at Hoy Field was played on April 22, 1922, against Colgate, and the first player to hit an outside-the-park home run was an opponent from Syracuse University. But the second home run, walloped by the starting pitcher and powerful left-handed hitter for the Columbia University team on April 21, 1923, remains the farthest ever hit here – according to witnesses, a distance of 450 feet from home plate.

The player's name was Henry Louis Gehrig, and later that year, baseball scout Paul Krichell was so impressed with the young man's hitting skills he was offered a $1,500 bonus and a contract with the New York Yankees. Lou Gehrig left Columbia and went on to become one of the greatest and most beloved players in baseball history, hitting a total of 493 home runs over fifteen seasons for the Yankees.

HOUDINI
APPEARS IN ITHACA

In 1916, Hereward Carrington, a well-known British investigator of the paranormal and author of such books as *Your Psychic Powers and How to Develop Them*, wrote a novel about the occult, which the Wharton Studio (see **Cliffhangers**, page 7) turned into a fifteen chapter serial called *The Mysteries of Myra*, filmed mostly in Ithaca.

To get the story right, the Whartons hired Carrington for costume ideas and set illustrations, as well as props such as pentagrams. As expert consultant for the unusual stunts (and for publicity value), the Whartons secured the services of Harry Houdini, legendary magician, escapologist (widely regarded as one of the greatest ever), and himself an investigator of psychic phenomena.

In the first episode, "The Secret Chamber," paranormal investigator Payson Alden sets out to help heroine Myra survive the evil Black Order's plot to destroy her with a hypnotic spell before she can inherit her father's fortune. The long-lost serial, distributed by Pathé Exchange, found a wide audience in an era of popular interest in secret societies and the occult.

ITHACA'S FIRST STARBUCK

In 1899, the player who led the Cornell football team to victory over Princeton (its first in the history of the rivalry) had nothing to do with coffee. Raymond Donald "Bucky" Starbuck, a kicking fullback from Glens Falls, was elected captain of the team in both 1899 and 1900, named as a consensus All-American in 1900. That year, sports writer Grantland Rice called him the "best man in football." After graduating from the College of Civil Engineering, Starbuck served as head coach during the 1901 and 1902 seasons (compiling a two-year record of 19-4) before accepting a job with the New York Central Railroad.

By 1917 Starbuck had climbed the ranks of the railroad's engineering department to become vice president of the lines from Buffalo to Chicago and St. Louis. After World War I, he was promoted to vice president of New York City lines, then in 1924, named as VP of operations. In 1932, Starbuck became the company's Executive VP, and in 1940 he replaced Walter P. Chrysler on the Board of Directors. He retired in 1949 and died in 1965 at age 87 in Rochester.

CHANGING TIMES

The twin 14-story residential towers on Ithaca College's South Hill campus have a commanding presence above the city, and since 1965 they have provided Ithacans a ceremonial light show to usher in the New Year. The tradition began as the brainchild of Petrus Van de Velde, former Assistant Supervisor of Custodial Services at the college.

For a few days before the holiday, lights in mapped-out windows of the towers are illuminated to spell out the current calendar year in 100-foot-high numerals. Special fixtures, originally with 300-watt incandescent bulbs (now with 100-watt fluorescents), are placed in the windows of student rooms (vacant over the holidays), and connected on each floor to a single power source, manned by as many as 25 volunteers from the college staff.

At the stroke of midnight on New Year's Eve, the towers' fire alarms are sounded as a signal, and in precisely coordinated teamwork, lights are turned on and off in the pre-determined rooms, instantly adjusting the display to mark the dawn of the New Year with its new number. Ithaca's version of the Times Square ball drop is a dramatic scene against the nighttime sky, visible for miles around.

THE PLAY'S THE THING

In another life, Ithaca's Hangar Theatre was a two-story glass, steel, and stone hangar that served Ithaca Municipal Airport (see **Wings Over Ithaca**, page 29), visited by Amelia Earhart who flew in during a lecture tour supporting sales of her autobiography. Its single short runway, proximity to the Lehigh Valley freight yards on the south side, lake marshes on the north side, and fog in the lake valley posed limits to growth, and in 1948 Cornell University opened the Ithaca Tompkins Regional Airport on East Hill, transferring ownership to the county in 1956.

With a grant from politician and philanthropist Nelson Rockefeller, the abandoned airport hangar was renovated in 1975 to become the home of the Center for the Arts at Ithaca. The inaugural season of the Hangar Theatre opened with a production of *Man of La Mancha*.

Over the years, productions have included performances by Billy Crudup (*Watchmen*), Amy Ryan (*Gone Baby Gone*), and Jimmy Smits (*West Wing*). Ithaca theatergoers have been able to say "I saw them when..."

EZRA'S SOCKS

In 1990, George David Low earned a bachelor of science degree in mechanical engineering from Cornell University and ten years later became a crew member on the thirty-third mission of America's Space Shuttle. On board the Orbiter Columbia, the crew successfully deployed the Syncom communications satellite, and retrieved the 21,400 -pound Long Duration Exposure Facility (LDEF) using a robotic arm. They also operated a variety of life science experiments, as well as the IMAX camera.

While Shuttle crew members are permitted to carry certain items of a personal nature on each flight, those items must be kept in the approved "Astronaut Preference Kit." Low took with him a pair of tan silk socks worn by Ezra Cornell on his wedding day in 1831. Then, in 1991, as the flight engineer aboard the Orbiter Atlantis, he brought another Ezra relic into space – the letter the founder wrote to his granddaughter expressing his wish that the university be coeducational. His father, George M. Low, was a former NASA director who was the first to suggest to President John F. Kennedy in 1960 that an astronaut could walk on the moon within the decade.

IMMORTAL SALOONKEEPER

A legendary Ithaca barkeep is immortalized in the Cornell fight song, "Give My Regards to Davy," with the following line: "We'll all have drinks at Theodore Zinck's, when I get back next fall!" In 1880, Zinck opened a "Lager Beer Saloon and Restaurant" in the Hotel Brunswick at 108-110 North Aurora Street. According to historian Morris Bishop, Zinck was a kindly, even fatherly German, "respectable to the marrow." He treated his lager and bock with reverence and his customers "with Prussian high-handedness." He allowed no drunkenness, bawdy songs, or derogatory references to the German Kaiser.

Zinck and his assistant, bartender Jimmy Griffin ("Jimmy De Griff"), were regarded with affection by generations of Cornellians. Zinck operated the business until his death in 1903. It was reopened at the same address in 1906, and continued intermittently under various names and at various sites until 1967.

On Dec. 3, 1884, the crowd at Zinck's was joined by Samuel Clemens (aka Mark Twain), who in an appearance at the local Wilgus Opera House, had recited passages from the novel that would be considered his masterpiece, *Adventures of Huckleberry Finn*.

ICE SKATING ACROSS CAYUGA

The longest of the Finger Lakes at nearly 40 miles, Cayuga measures 435 feet at its deepest point. Its average width is 1.7 miles, and 3.5 miles wide at its widest point near Aurora. Its depth, steep east and west sides with shallow north and south ends is typical of the Finger Lakes, carved by glaciers during the last ice age (see **Prehistoric Ithaca**, page 99). The water level is regulated by the Mud Lock at the north end of the lake, drawn down as winter approaches to minimize ice damage and to maximize its capacity to store heavy spring runoff.

A well-documented Wells College tradition holds that when the lake freezes over, the college president declares a school holiday. With classes canceled in 1875, student Emma Lampert skated across the lake and back. Six weeks of excessive cold preceded the freezing during the winter of 1912. Ice twenty-two to twenty-four inches thick formed in the shallows at both ends of the lake, and as the cold weather continued, the frozen area gradually extended outward. During the night of February 10, the wind subsided, and the morning of the 11th found Cayuga Lake frozen from end to end.

FREE THE AIRWAVES!

In 1903, experimental signals sent over the airwaves by a handful of Cornell electrical engineers were prelude to what is now one of the oldest radio stations in North America, WHCU (for "Home of Cornell University"). On June 30, 1935, the station became one of the first affiliates of the fledgling Columbia Broadcasting System (CBS). Early programming had an emphasis on education, agriculture, lectures, drama, and sports, along with live and recorded music. Dozens of professors and locals had their own programs on everything from flying to photography, birds to bowling, gardening to ham radio.

WHCU remained in the university's hands until 1985, when it was sold to Eagle Broadcasting. Then, in early 2001, radio mega-corporation Saga Communications of Grosse Point Farms, Michigan, acquired WHCU, issuing a press release promising "to continue the great heritage that the station has established." Instead, Saga instituted a dramatic change of format that could only be described as counter-intuitive. WHCU became the "right-wing noise machine" in one of America's most liberal cities, with syndicated programming that includes Laura Ingraham, Rush Limbaugh, Sean Hannity, and Mark Levin.

AMERICAN NEWSBOY

A man who carved out an empire in America's newspaper world was born in 1876 on a small farm in South Bristol in Ontario County. Frank Ernest Gannett peddled papers as a boy and worked his way through Cornell as a cub reporter for the *Ithaca Journal*. After graduating in 1898, he became the *Journal*'s managing editor, business manager, and by 1912, its owner. In 1918, he bought two Rochester newspapers and by the end of the 1920, owned 15 dailies in New York and other papers in New Jersey, Connecticut and Illinois.

Active in politics, Gannett arrived in Philadelphia with three circus elephants to attend the 1940 Republican Convention but lost his bid for the presidential nomination to corporate lawyer Wendell Wilkie. During his lifetime, Frank Gannett amassed a publishing group of 22 newspapers in 18 cities. He owned four radio stations and three television stations. Today, the company is the country's largest newspaper group with 95 daily newspapers, including national publication *USA Today*.

Among his philanthropic gifts, Gannett donated half a million dollars for the construction of the Gannett Health Center at Cornell.

LOCAL HEROES

Neighboring cities of Auburn and Cortland produced two of Cornell's greatest football players. After graduating from Auburn High School, Jerome "Brud" Holland became the first African American to play on the Cornell football team. He was also one of the greatest college football players of his era, an excellent two-way end known for his end-around plays as a three-year starter on the teams of 1936, 1937 and 1938. He was a first-team All-American in both 1937 and 1938 and was inducted into the National Football Foundation Hall of Fame in 1965. Holland went on to become president of Hampton Institute. After serving as the United States ambassador to Sweden, he became the first African-American director of the New York Stock Exchange.

Cornell's greatest-ever quarterback, Gary Wood, was raised by a single mom in Cortland. After graduating from Cortland High School, he went on to wear number "19" as Cornell's three-year starting quarterback beginning in 1961, leading the team in rushing and passing every year. In 1964 he was drafted by the New York Giants in the eighth round, backing up the legendary Y. A. Tittle and frequently thrilling crowds with his fearless rollout style and his penchant for turning planned handoffs into impromptu bootleg plays for big gains.

ITHACA'S ROYAL FAMILY

Selected by none other than George Washington himself to accompany both General Anthony Wayne in his attack on Stony Point and Major General John Sullivan in his Indian Expedition (see **"Noble Savages,"** page 18), Abner Treman was handsomely rewarded for his war service with 600 acres of land in what is now Trumansburg. The village was named after the family, but in making out his commission, the postmaster misspelled "Tremansburg," and so it has remained.

Abner's descendants made their marks as entrepreneurs in Ithaca, first entering the hardware business (Treman, King & Co.) in a building that occupied the entire block of South Cayuga Street, from State to Green. Eventually, the family controlled the local Water Works and Gas Light Company, operated mills, served as officers of local banks and trustees of the university, and became active public figures.

As the wealthiest Ithacans, the Tremans owned some the area's most treasured land, and in 1920, Abner's grandson, Robert H. Treman, donated a 387-acre parcel in Enfield Glen to the state for the development of a public park.

CORNELL
SPELLED BACKWARDS

In 1867, Ezra Cornell began construction of a sprawling mansion he called "Llenroc" (the backwards spelling of his name) on a knoll overlooking Ithaca and Cayuga Lake. He hired an Albany firm, Nichols and Brown, to design a plan which borrowed heavily from both Gothic and High Victorian styles. German artisans were commissioned to carve elaborate designs into the native bluestone (see **The Stone That Built Cornell**, page 55), hauled from a quarry just west of White Hall on the Arts Quad, while English artisans were hired to carve the woodwork. Eight complete marble fireplaces were imported from Europe and placed throughout the house. Irish, Scottish, and Italian immigrants, as well as Native Americans, were employed as laborers.

The phrase "True and Firm" was carved over the entryway at the suggestion of university president Andrew Dickson White. Sadly, Ezra did not get to live in his dream house. He died in 1874, a year before the mansion was completed. Ownership of Llenroc remained in the Cornell family until 1911, when the house was purchased by the Delta Phi fraternity.

ITHACA'S FOUNDING FATHER

The physician's son was sent to Queens (Rutgers) College in New Brunswick, New Jersey, where he was its only graduate in 1776. Trained as a surveyor, Simeon DeWitt joined the Continental army, eventually named Geographer-in-Chief, assigned to General Washington's headquarters. While serving as Surveyor General of New York State, he acquired 1,400 acres of land at the headwaters of Cayuga Lake from his father-in-law, Abraham Bloodgood, who took possession after rights of the Cayuga tribe were extinguished. DeWitt had a subdivision survey made and offered lots for sale.

He named his land "Ithaca," first noted on a map of 1807. In the late 1810s, he sold about half of the Publick Square (what is now DeWitt Park) to the Presbyterian Church. In 1856, the city took over the care and control of the park, but the church retained the title, an agreement still in force. During DeWitt's later years he moved into the Clinton House (see **Saved from the Wrecking Ball**, page 82) and resided there until his death in 1834. He was buried on his estate, but his remains were later moved to Albany, interred at Albany Rural Cemetery.

GRATEFUL ITHACA

From the band's inception, the Grateful Dead toured practically nonstop, and in as many as 2,300 performances over their 30-year career, they never played the same set twice. For that matter, they never played a song the same way twice, instead relaxing traditional song structure in order to allow for extended improvisational jams. It often worked remarkably well, and according to legend, it never worked better than on the night of May 8, 1977, in Cornell's Barton Hall.

That concert is widely regarded by many to be the best single gig the band ever played, in the words of former Mayor Carolyn Peterson in recognition of the thirtieth anniversary of the event, "a defining and transcendent occasion and example of the art of contemporary musical improvisation, collaboration, musicianship, and performance." As an undergraduate, Jeffrey S. Lehman, the first alumnus of Cornell to serve as its president, was in charge of ticket sales and concessions for the concert.

Over the years bootleg tapes, including revelatory performances of "Scarlet Begonias," "Fire on the Mountain," and "Morning Dew," have taken on legendary stature.

PATH TO ENLIGHTENMENT

Since 1959, natives of Tibet have scattered throughout the world, fleeing the Communist Chinese occupation of their country. Among the first Tibetan refugees to arrive in Ithaca in 1992 was a monk from Namgyal, the Dalai Lama's monastery in Dharamsala, India. With his inspiration and the help of American friends, a modest house on Aurora Street was transformed into a cultural and religious center for the Tibetan community, growing to become the North American seat of His Holiness the 14th Dalai Lama, personally blessed during his visit to Ithaca in 2007.

In addition to the downtown location, Namgyal has established a retreat center and monastery on Route 96-B, offering students an opportunity to study the Tibetan Buddhist tradition. Visiting faculty include prominent western scholars, clergy, and teachers from all traditions. Ithaca is also the home of Snow Lion, a highly influential Tibetan Buddhist publishing company that came into being after the Dalai Lama made his first visit to the United States in 1980. The Tibetan national flag is flown daily on the Ithaca Commons.

KING'S ROW

On Martin Luther King Jr. Day, January 19, 2009, the City of Ithaca unveiled the dual designation of Martin Luther King/State Street, and in 2012, a sculpture connecting Dr. King to Ithaca (created by local artist Rob Licht) was installed on the Commons (see **No-Car Zone**, page 56).

Dr. King first visited Ithaca in November 1960, arriving on the Lehigh Valley Railroad. He had breakfast with Cornell students at the Statler Hotel, gave a sermon to a standing-room-only congregation in Sage Chapel, then answered questions from a crowd gathered in the Memorial Room of Willard Straight Hall. It was King's last appearance in the United States before his historic trip to Nigeria, a country then celebrating its newfound independence from Great Britain. King flew directly from Ithaca to New York and from there to Africa.

He returned to Ithaca in April 1961 to speak at a fundraiser in Bailey Hall, invited by the Cornell Committee Against Segregation, chaired by Dr. Edward Hart, a local ophthalmologist. In his speech, Dr. King explained, "It is human dignity which we are struggling for, and we still have a long, long way to go."

How to Lick "Old Man Depression"

America's Great Depression began with a catastrophic collapse of stock-market prices on the New York Stock Exchange in October 1929. With 25 to 30 percent of the country's work force unemployed, President Franklin Roosevelt created the Civilian Conservation Corps as a public work relief program, focused on natural resource conservation of national, state and municipal lands. From 1933 to 1941, a C.C.C. camp was established in Enfield, near the Old Mill at Upper Treman Park.

More than 100 young men wore uniforms, and lived under quasi-military discipline, first in tents and later in wooden barracks complete with mess and recreation halls, and shower and infirmary buildings. The men of the C.C.C. camp improved many of the region's trails, quarried and cut the stone for walkways throughout the area's parks. The local camp was declared the winner in a contest with 23 other camps throughout New York and New Jersey based on conduct, morale, application to camp life, camp arrangement and routine. Initials and names of some of these men inscribed in the cliff walls may be found in various places in the glen, often with the letters "C.C.C."

USED BOOKS FOR LESS

The Friends of the Library Booksale is a twice-annual local fundraiser, on a scale that makes it the third largest event of its kind in America. Since 1946, Friends of the Library has given more than three million dollars to the Tompkins County Public Library and more than a half million dollars to the Finger Lakes Library System. For each event, volunteers fill a warehouse on Esty Street with as many as 250,000 community-donated books, magazines, puzzles, games, video and audio cassettes, CDs, and vinyl albums.

Sale dates, beginning in October and again in April or May, take place over two weeks, with prices of items continually decreasing until the final day when one can purchase a supermarket bag full of books for one dollar. Early birds have been known to camp outside of the warehouse before the first day of the sale. While most are local bibliophiles adding to private collections, the sale attracts used book dealers who purchase items at bargain prices for markup and resale. For this reason, buyers are limited to fifty purchases per visit on the first day of the sale. At the end of the sale, leftover materials are donated to non-profit organizations, teachers, and home schoolers.

RETIREMENT FOR THE WELL-HEELED

Named for a congregation of Quaker families in 18th century England, the Kendal Corporation, founded with a grant from the Religious Society of Friends, develops retirement communities that operate in accordance with its Quaker roots and principles. In 1995, Kendal at Ithaca, built on a 105-acre site known locally as Savage Farm, became the first "continuing care" retirement community to open in New York State.

A Kendal applicant must be at least 65 years old, active and ambulatory, with no serious health problems, and reasonably expected to continue that way for the first year in order to join the community. He or she must be eligible for Medicare, pay a non-refundable "entry fee" roughly equivalent to the purchase of a quality home, although the condominium-style apartment remains the property of the corporation. A retirement plan or investment portfolio is expected to pay substantial monthly fees for group health care, meals, and long-term care. The community emphasizes independent living and resident participation in setting policies for the facilities.

 # BO KNOWS BURGERS

Before the late 1960s, the term "counter culture" in Ithaca referred to something other than social progressives and political activists. Late night social life led to a diner on West State Street called Obie's, a domed, railroad car-shaped gathering place with ten seats at the counter and two tables. Obie's was the home of the Bo-Burger, a combination allegedly devised in the early '50s for Bo Roberson, Cornell's All-America football player, the only person ever to earn an Ivy League degree, an Olympic medal, and a doctorate, while going on to an NFL career (he was the Oakland Raiders' most valuable player in 1962).

The culinary masterpiece consisted of a hamburger topped with finely-diced, sauteed onions, fried egg with a broken yolk, and melted cheese. A midnight run to Obie's could also include a hash-brown potato patty and if you were still hungry, an apple turnover, warmed on the grill and smeared with butter. Bo-Burgers were very good to proprietor Obie, who sold enough of them to buy a new Cadillac every year and vacation every July and August in Spain.

Another local masterpiece, the Tullyburger (grilled cheeseburger with raw onions, lettuce, tomato and mayonnaise) originated at Wes and Les's, across from the old Lehigh Valley station.

THE STONE
THAT BUILT CORNELL

The sand-size grains that make up "bluestone," deposited during the Devonian Period of the Paleozoic Era, roughly 345 to 370 million years ago, were formed as a result of erosion of the Acadian Mountains, the ancestral name for the present-day Appalachians. This origin has influenced bluestone's mineral composition, making it very durable. It is resistant to wear, changes in temperature, and shifts in pressure. It also splits easily into manageable layers with relative ease, making it ideal for use as architectural and building stone.

The bluestone of this region, exclusive to south-central New York and northeast Pennsylvania, cannot be found commercially anywhere else in the United States or Canada. The majority of the blue or bluish-gray stone quarried from narrow veins in what is now the base of Cornell's Libe slope provided the primary building material for the elegant buildings of the Arts Quad. Morrill Hall, the first university building to be constructed on campus, together with White Hall and McGraw Hall are known as "Stone Row." Ezra Cornell used local bluestone in the construction his grand villa, "Llenroc" (see **Cornell Spelled Backwards**, page 46).

NO-CAR ZONE

Ithaca's earliest business district developed along Owego Street, the main thoroughfare and stagecoach route through the village. Originally, the street turned at its eastern end, then headed up South Hill, connecting to the Ithaca-Owego Turnpike. In 1867, the name was changed to State Street by village proclamation. A century later, at a time when many small downtowns around the country were facing competition from enclosed suburban malls, the City of Ithaca began discussing how to reverse its own commercial decline.

By 1974, two central blocks of State Street, between Aurora Street on the east and Cayuga Street on the west, were closed to vehicular traffic, as trees, benches, sculptures, and pavilions were added. It was the first locally planned and funded pedestrian mall in New York State, an attempt to compete with malls outside the city. "The Commons" was the winning entry in a community-wide "name the mall" contest, and a prize of $1,000 went to Ithaca High School senior Bill Ryan.

While most of the outside pedestrian malls around the country proved unsuccessful, Ithaca Commons is one of few such experiments that still remain, an oasis amidst the one-way streets of Ithaca.

GOING SIDEWAYS INTO HISTORY

According to to local legend, football's soccer-style placekicking movement began in Ithaca. Many folks are under the impression that Pete Gogolak, pride of Cornell, was the first sidewinder (as they were called in those days), striking the ball with his instep.

A native of Budapest, Hungary, Gogolak settled in Ogdensburg in 1956 after his family fled the Hungarian Revolution. His high school didn't have a soccer team, so Gogolak put his skills to work in football, going on to play for Cornell, the AFL's Buffalo Bills, and the NFL's New York Giants. Gogolak made a name for himself in 1963 by kicking the first-ever 50-yard field goal at Schoellkopf Field and by setting a record for the most consecutive extra-point conversions (44).

As pro football's first soccer-style kicker, Gogolak permanently influenced the game, but it was Fred Bednarski, a Polish refugee playing for the University of Texas Longhorns, who booted college football's first soccer-style field goal on October 19, 1957, a distance of 38-yard against the Arkansas Razorbacks.

# Rags to Riches

The second eldest of nine children from a working-class Irish Catholic neighborhood in nearby Elmira, Thomas Jacob Hilfiger attended Elmira Free Academy. While still in high school, Tommy would trek down to New York City and bring back odd-lot jeans to sell out of an Elmira basement. In 1975, he opened a store on Aurora Street in downtown Ithaca called "People's Place," and although he had no formal training, he designed vests and sweaters to supplement jeans and bell-bottoms. The store was poorly managed, and in 1977, Tommy was forced to declare bankruptcy.

He picked up the pieces and headed to New York City with wife Susan (who he met when she applied for a job at the Ithaca store). As luck would have it, Mohan Murjani, license holder of Gloria Vanderbilt jeans, offered to back Tommy's start-up company, and within a year Tommy Hilfiger, Inc. went public, extending into 40 product lines, including fragrances, belts, bedding, home furnishings, and cosmetics. Twenty years later the company had 5,400 employees and revenues in excess of 1.8 billion dollars. In 2006, Tommy sold his company for 1.6 billion dollars to a private investment company, Apax Partners.

WEST HILL UTOPIA

In 1990, on a pilgrimage from Los Angeles to New York City to raise awareness about the environment, activist Joan Bokaer came up with an idea for building an "ecological city," eventually settling on a 176-acre parcel of farm fields, wetlands, and woods on Ithaca's West Hill to create what is now an internationally-known sustainable community. Less than 2 miles from downtown and served by the local bus system, EcoVillage aspires to integrate the best aspects of urban and rural living.

Its houses, all duplexes to save energy, are privately owned by the residents, who pay a monthly fee for the upkeep of common buildings. They share laundry machines, babysitters, TVs, even cars. The village includes an organic CSA vegetable farm, a warm-season grasses ecosystem restoration project, a sheep pasture, and varied natural areas. Residents share common dinners several times per week in Common Houses and volunteer time for outdoor maintenance, finances, governance, and future projects.

Past visitors have gone on to start their own EcoVillages in Vermont and Virginia.

VEGETARIANS IN PARADISE

Bon Appetit magazine ranks Ithaca's own Moosewood as one of the most influential restaurants of the twentieth century, at the forefront of a movement that has had a profound impact on the American diet. Founded by seven original members in 1973, Moosewood became a wellspring for a number of vegetarian cookbooks, but not without controversy. The original *Moosewood Cookbook* by Molly Katzen included pen-and-ink illustrations and hand-lettered recipes she claims were developed without participation of the restaurant collective.

First produced in an un-bylined, spiral-bound booklet, it was discovered by Philip Wood of then-fledgeling Ten Speed Press who first recognized the potential of a groundbreaking vegetarian cookbook. Katzen's association with the restaurant had long since lapsed when Wood signed Katzen to a contract that excluded members of the group from receiving any royalties, as well as prohibiting publication of their own books using the Moosewood name, for a period of several years. Katzen's *Moosewood Cookbook* went on to become one of the best-selling cookbooks of all time. Since the restriction was lifted, the Moosewood collective has produced a series of its own cookbooks.

SODOM ON CAYUGA

During its frontier days, Ithaca was called the "Evil City" or just plain "Sodom," after the Biblical city of sin, a reputation earned by the town's penchant for horseracing, gambling, profanity, Sabbath breaking, and readily available liquor. Disrepute was further buoyed by establishment of Ithaca's "godless university," a reference to Cornell's lack of affiliation with any organized religion, radical for an institution of higher learning at the time.

With the opening of the Erie Canal and building of the railroads, Ithaca was connected to more of the outside world, and with economic boom came successive waves of gamblers, bootleggers, prostitutes, and con artists, many settling in the rough and rowdy West End. That part of town became known as the "Silent City," since residents were always tight-lipped whenever the police came to investigate a reported crime. Patrolling the West End was called "Watch on the Rhine," and respectable Ithacans stayed away at night. Passengers who arrived on the Black Diamond (see **The Handsomest Train in the World**, page 75) were quickly whisked from the West End railroad station to a more civilized part of town.

LET THEM EAT CAKE

In 1942, young Roy Park arrived in Ithaca to run an advertising agency, with H.E. Babcock's Grange League Federation (see **Experimental Farm**, page 85) as its main client. Seeking premium branding for GLF's food products, Park convinced Duncan Hines, well-known author of *Adventures in Good Eating*, to lend his name to the labels. The resulting company, Hines-Park Foods, was a stunning success, especially with its flagship product, Duncan Hines Cake Mix. Only five years after releasing its first products, Hines-Park was acquired by Procter & Gamble.

That 1956 buyout helped finance Park's media acquisitions, and over three decades he built an empire of 11 television stations, 22 radio stations and 144 newspapers – a market that reached one-quarter of all American households. By 1993 he was listed by *Forbes* as the 40th richest man in America. He lived the remainder of his life in Ithaca, and upon his death in 1993, bequeathed his holdings to the Park Foundation, in support of education, public broadcasting, environment, and other areas of interest to the Park family.

Senator Sam Ervin once said, "Park is one of the finest human beings the good Lord ever created."

VIRGIN DETECTORS

On the East Hill Arts Quad, the site of Cornell's original academic buildings, a statue of founder Ezra Cornell (see **Surplus Wealth**, page 8) stands between McGraw Hall and Morrill Hall, and a statue of the university's first president, Andrew Dickson White, sits upon a chair in front of Goldwin Smith Hall. According to campus folklore, if a virgin crosses the quad as the clock tower strikes midnight, the statues will walk off their pedestals, meet in the center, and shake hands, congratulating each other on the chastity of the university. The legend is memorialized by a trail of footprints, first painted in 1927 by Hugh Troy (see **Rhinoceros Drowns in Beebe Lake**, page 13), Ithaca's legendary practical joker, and repainted every year since.

On the roof plaza of Ithaca College's Textor Hall stands "Disc," sculptor Jack Squier's 10-foot high, round metal interpretation of a fish, mounted over a small pool of water, and referred to by students as the "Textor Ball." It is said that when a virgin graduates from IC, the Textor Ball will roll off its pedestal and all the way down the hill. It has never moved.

POP CULTURE

Cornell has been referenced over 30 times in the TV quiz show *Jeopardy*, and at least twice in "Final Jeopardy." Alex Trebek once provided this answer: "Older than his classmates, Cornell football player and future coach Glenn Warner got this nickname." The question, answered correctly, was "What was 'Pop'?"

Upon witnessing his first football game in 1890, Warner thought it "just a schoolboy scramble with a few bloody noses." He went on to captain the Big Red football team. As a coach for his alma mater, he accumulated a solid 36-13-1 record, and at the University of Pittsburgh he compiled 33 straight victories and two national championships. He also won three Rose Bowl championships as head coach of the Stanford Cardinals.

After the 1905 season, when 15 collegiate players were killed playing the game, Warner became a leading advocate of new safety rules and equipment. His other innovations included the body block, screen play, single- and double-wing formations, spiral forward pass, and the crouching three-point stance. His legacy is the Pop Warner Football League, founded in 1929, the nation's oldest and largest youth football organization.

IN ITHACA WE TRUST

The concept of Ithaca Hours, introduced in 1991 by local activist Paul Glover, is a form of barter currency, utilizing paper notes traded among residents and businesses, including the Cayuga Medical Center, Alternatives Federal Credit Union, the public library, farmers, movie theatres, restaurants, massage therapists, plumbers, carpenters, electricians, and landlords as legal tender. One Ithaca "Hour" is meant to be equivalent to an hour's worth of labor, with the exact rate of exchange for any given transaction decided by the parties themselves.

Proudhon socialists have long argued for a system of "labour money" to correct the unfairness of capitalism. As a local medium of exchange, Ithaca Hours establish labor as the true measure of value in our community. Millions of dollars worth of transactions have taken place using the currency, and the Ithaca Hours system has become both the subject of academic studies and a model for community currency systems worldwide, bringing observers to Ithaca, including Danielle Mitterrand (former first lady of France) and community development specialists from every continent.

In 2014, Ithacash replaced Ithaca Hours as the community money system.

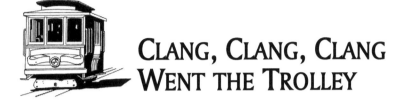

CLANG, CLANG, CLANG WENT THE TROLLEY

Following Brooklyn and Binghamton, Ithaca was the third city in New York State to install an electric trolley system. In 1887, the first track was laid, extending from the West End railroad station to the Ithaca Hotel (a re-created section of the original trolley track is visible at the center of Ithaca Commons). In 1892, threatened with competition for passengers, horse-drawn carriage operators hired an engineering school professor from Cornell to declare that trolleys could not possibly climb East Hill. But climb they did, powered by hydroelectricity from Six Mile Creek, Cascadilla and Fall Creeks.

On a 1900 campaign trip to Ithaca, New York Governor and vice presidential candidate Teddy Roosevelt was transported from Cornell into downtown in a decorated trolley car, cheered by Ithacans of all ages from porches and lawns along the way. In 1914, a trolley car provided the most famous single scene ever filmed in Ithaca (see **Cliffhangers**, page 7) with a plunge off the Stewart Avenue bridge over Fall Creek gorge during the Wharton brothers' filming of *The Kiss of Blood*. 1935 marked the end of the trolley era in Ithaca.

LOST IN TIME

DECEMBER						
S	M	T	W	T	F	S
..	..	..	..	..	..	1
2	3	4	5	6	7	8
9	10	11	12	13	14	15
16	17	18	19	20	21	22
23	24	25	26	27	28	29
30	31	..	..	..	..	..

The first calendar operated by clock machinery was invented in Ithaca by J. H. Hawes, who secured a patent in 1853. His clever timepiece perpetually indicated the day of the month, month of the year, hour of the day, and day of the week. The Ithaca Calendar Clock Company was established in 1865, improving the original model with a perpetual roller-type calendar, adjusting automatically to accommodate a Leap Year. The clock faces on the Ithaca clocks were made up of two circular dials, one above the other, with time indicated on the top dial and the day of the week and the month of the year on the bottom dial.

The company quickly outgrew an early location on State Street, eventually erecting factory buildings on the old Tompkins County Fairgrounds at the intersection of Adams, Auburn, Dey and Franklin Streets. At the peak of prosperity, the Ithaca Calendar Clock Company produced 6,000 clocks a year, in forty different styles and combinations, selling around the world at prices ranging from $10 to $75 each. The company's demise in 1920 was due in most part to Prohibition, since a large part of the company's business came from brewers and distributors, who gave away the clocks as premiums to their customers.

EAST HILL CLIMBERS

Many alumni have made their mark in what the *Cornell Sun* called the "Great Outside World." They include actors Frank Morgan (who played Professor Marvel in 1939's *The Wizard of Oz*), Franchot Tone, Dane Clark, Adolphe Menjou, Christopher Reeve, Jimmy Smits, Gardner McKay, and Mary Woronov; movie director Howard Hawks; writers include E. B. White, Toni Morrison, Kurt Vonnegut, Pearl Buck, Thomas Pynchon, Tom Peters, Ken Blanchard, Murray Burnett, Richard Farina, and Clifford Irving; journalists include Margaret Bourke-White, Charles Collingwood, Dick Schaap, Keith Olbermann, Dave Ross, Kate Snow, and Ann Coulter; musicians include Laurens Hammond, Robert Moog, Peter Yarrow, Harry Chapin, and Huey Lewis; entrepreneurs Charles Feeney, Sanford Weill, Willis Carrier Adolph Coors, Leroy Grumman, Frank Gannett, David Edgerton, and Jay Walker; others notables include Henry Heimlich, Robert Trent Jones, Allen Funt, Bill Nye, Art Fleming, Bill Maher, Joyce Brothers, Ricky Jay, Ken Dryden, Ed Marinaro, Ruth Bader Ginsburg, Janet Reno, William P. Rogers, Ed Muskie, Mark Green, Alan Keyes, Chuck Robb, Sandy Berger, Stephen Hadley, Paul Wolfowitz, David Augustus Embury, and Drew Nieporent.

SOUTH HILL CLIMBERS

Former Ithaca College students include Robert Allen Iger, who earned a Bachelor of Science degree in Television & Radio (Magna Cum Laude) from the Park School of Communications. After graduation he became the weatherman at ABC's New York affiliate. He rose through the ranks at ABC to become president of the company in 1994 and the Disney Company's second in command six years later (Disney bought ABC in 1995.) In 2005, he succeeded Michael Eisner to become Disney's CEO, "Ruler of the Magic Kingdom." In 2008, Iger earned a total compensation of $51,072,580.

Other former students include Jessica Savitch, the first female network anchor; Les Otten vice-chairman and partner of the Boston Red Sox Organization; James W. Bates, writer on *The Simpsons*; Bob Kur, national NBC reporter; Barbara Gaines, Emmy Award-winning executive producer (*Late Show with David Letterman*); actor Gavin MacLeod (*The Love Boat* and *The Mary Tyler Moore Show*); actor David Boreanaz (Seeley Booth on crime drama *Bones*); Thomas F.X. Beusse, president of Westwood One; and director David Rogers (*The Office*).

KISS AND TELL

As an engineering student at Cornell in 1889, Edward Wyckoff drew up plans for the first suspension bridge spanning Fall Creek gorge as a course project. Twenty years later, Wyckoff, heir to the Remington typewriter fortune, financed the construction of his bridge, an eyebar chain suspension structure with a swaying, 5 1/2 foot-wide plank walkway. The original bridge is immortalized in Lyman H. Howe's two-reel feature film, *The Hermit of Lonely Gulch* (see **Cliffhangers**, page 7).

The present suspension bridge was designed by S.C. Hollister, Dean of Engineering, and Professor William McGuire, an expert on structural collapses. The construction contract was awarded to Bethlehem Steel Company, builders of the Golden Gate and George Washington Bridges. It was opened for use on January 7, 1961, with close-spaced, prison-style bars as deterrent to 138-foot leaps into the gorge. (Contrary to popular notion, the suicide rate at Cornell is below the national average).

Campus legend claims that refusing a midnight kiss while crossing the suspension bridge will cause the span to crumble and drop into the gorge.

SEINFELD IN ITHACA

"Good afternoon, Ithaca, welcome. Good to see you here," says Jerry Seinfeld. It was the 108th episode of TV sitcom *Seinfeld*, called "The Diplomat's Club" (season 6), in which Jerry's assistant Katie (Debra Jo Rupp) makes his trip to Ithaca a nightmare.

She invites the pilot of his flight to see his standup act. A tightly wound control freak, she makes Jerry nervous for his set by saying that the pilot's presence in the audience shouldn't make him nervous, which of course makes him extremely nervous, and causes him to perform poorly.

Katie harangues the pilot, and when Jerry tries to fly back to New York, the same pilot throws him off the plane.

# NICKNAMES

During his senior year at Cornell in 1905, Romeyn "Rym" Berry composed the lyrics for a song called "The Big Red Team," thereby dubbing Cornell athletic teams the Big Red. (Berry later served as the Graduate Director of Cornell Athletics). A live bear named "Touchdown" became the Cornell mascot during the 1915 national championship football season, a position held by three other bears, one of whom was abducted by Harvard, until replaced by a costumed undergraduate in 1939. A bronze statue in the likeness of a bear cub was installed outside Teagle Hall in 2015.

Ithaca College teams were named the "Cayugans," until an *Ithaca Journal* sports columnist started calling them the "Bombers." He claimed the school's pinstriped baseball uniforms bore a striking resemblance to the uniforms of the New York Yankees (the "Bronx Bombers"), and by in 1938 the new nickname had stuck. Unique in NCAA athletics, the name has at times sparked controversy for its military connotation, especially during the period when a World War II-era fighter plane was incorporated in the logo, but the athletics department has consistently stated it has no interest in changing the name.

FARM BOY VICE PRESIDENT

Daniel D. Tompkins was born in what is now Scarsdale in Westchester County on June 21, 1774, one of eleven children of tenant farmers Jonathan Griffin Tompkins and Sarah Ann Hyatt Tompkins. He was baptized Daniel Tompkins, but added the middle initial "D" while a student at Columbia University to distinguish himself from a fellow student named Daniel Tompkins.

He earned a law degree from Columbia, and in 1797 was admitted to the bar, establishing a practice in New York City. He was a delegate to the New York State Constitutional Convention in 1801, a member of the New York State Assembly in 1803, and was elected to the United States Congress, but resigned before the beginning of the term to accept an appointment as associate justice of the Supreme Court of New York. In 1807, he defeated incumbent Morgan Lewis to become Governor of New York, and in 1816 was elected Vice President of the United States on the ticket with James Monroe.

Although Daniel Tompkins never set foot here, the state of New York named the county for him in 1817.

BEST REGARDS

A year after composer George M. Cohan popularized "Give My Regards to Broadway" in the musical comedy *Little Johnny Jones*, a trio of roommates from Beta Theta Pi house, Charles E. Tourison, W. L. Umstad, and Bill Forbes, re-wrote the lyrics over beers at Zinck's (see **Immortal Saloonkeeper**, page 40) and re-named the song "Give My Regards to Davy."

The Cornell-inspired version refers to a fictional encounter between a "piker," (slang term for a freshman), David Fletcher "Davy" Hoy, the university registrar and secretary for the committee on student conduct, and Thomas Frederick "Tee Fee" Crane, the first Dean of the College of Arts and Sciences. The student, having been expelled for drinking, states his determination to return in the fall, both to studies and to the local saloon. Notorious for his strict sense of discipline, Hoy was also a bench coach for the baseball team (see **Longest Home Run**, page 34). Professor Crane, on the other hand, was usually more lenient and well-liked among students.

"Give My Regards to Davy" became the official Cornell University fight song, performed by the Big Red Marching Band during athletic contests.

HANDSOMEST TRAIN
IN THE WORLD

Originally chartered in 1846 as a transporter of coal from the anthracite fields of Pennsylvania, the Lehigh Valley Railroad grew into a major carrier of both freight and passengers between Buffalo and New York City. Its first connection to Ithaca began in 1885 with the construction of a passenger station in the West End, eventually serving as many as eighteen trains per day, including the luxurious, 315-foot-long Black Diamond Express, pulled by a Pacific-type steam locomotive painted "Cornell Red."

Its dining compartment was served by a corps of skilled chefs. Streamlined coaches were finished in polished mahogany, with carved panels and beveled French plate mirrors, outfitted with plush velvet chairs, a large comfortable smoking room, and lavatories for both men and women. The Pullman Palace Car seated 28 passengers and included a parlor and an observation platform. Because of its appeal to newlyweds on their way to Niagara Falls, the train was nicknamed the "Honeymoon Express."

The run of the Black Diamond ended in 1959, and passenger service to Ithaca ended entirely in 1961. Fifteen miles of the abandoned Lehigh Valley rail corridor has been dedicated to an off-road pedestrian and bicycle trail.

FOR WHOM
THE BELL RINGS

William A. Anthony, who arrived in Ithaca in 1872 to teach physics at Cornell, invented a ring-armature dynamo used to light the campus. It was the first electrical generator built in this country, and it powered an arc light strung between McGraw Hall and Sage Chapel – the earliest outdoor application of its kind in the world. While attending the Philadelphia Centennial Exposition in 1876 to exhibit his dynamo, Professor Anthony met Alexander Graham Bell, who was there to demonstrate an early telephone prototype. Bell encouraged Anthony to establish a telephone exchange in Ithaca, and by 1880, the local system connected 100 subscribers. (Until the 1950s, Ithaca had the largest number of telephones per capita of any city in America).

The first telephone lines used a single wire system, with coded rings to signal parties on a party line. With the introduction of a two-wire system, it became possible to selectively ring one half or the other by applying ringing voltage to the correct wire. It was in Ithaca where "divided ringing" began, eliminating the need for a call to ring at every instrument. For the first time anywhere, each party heard only his own rings.

CRASHING THE BOY'S CLUB

In the early years of Cornell, the Board of Trustees reflected the view of many Ithacans who were opposed to co-education, fearing that it would lead women astray from the path of "true womanhood." They declared it "contrary to nature," "likely to produce confusion," and "dangerous."

As they were both traveling by steamboat (see **Golden Age of Paddleboats**, page 96) across Cayuga Lake in 1868, suffragette Emily Howland happened to meet Ezra Cornell, and used the opportunity to plant the seed for the creation of the university as a co-educational institution. Other proponents of women's rights, including Susan B. Anthony, wrote to Ezra Cornell urging him to open the university to women.

In the fall of 1870, Cortland native Jennie Spencer was the first woman to register at Cornell. She boarded in town and, dressed in long skirts and petticoats, trudged through cow pastures and over fences to attend classes. With the arrival of winter, the back and forth became unbearable and she withdrew, her semester unfinished. Three years later, Emma Sheffield Eastman, who had transferred from Vassar, became the university's first female graduate.

THE SON ALSO RISES

Beginning in 1923, secondary education in Ithaca took place at Ithaca Academy, a preparatory school supported by tuition fees. The private school made the transition into a public school (Ithaca High School) in the fall of 1875. Among graduates sent out into the world by Ithaca Academy were professors, judges, congressmen, and in one case, the Governor of the State.

Alonzo Barton Cornell, the eldest son of Ezra Cornell and Ithaca Academy graduate, became director of the Western Union Telegraph Company, pioneered by his father. Afterwards, he owned commercial steamboats on Cayuga Lake. From 1864 to 1869 he was an officer of the First National Bank of Ithaca and Supervisor of the Town of Ithaca. He served as chairman of the Tompkins County Republican Committee and as a member of the Republican State Committee. President Ulysses S. Grant appointed Mr. Cornell Surveyor of Customs at the Port of New York, a position he resigned to become a member of the State Assembly in 1873. Alonzo Cornell was elected Governor of New York, but ten years later, after a series of poor investments, he returned to Ithaca nearly broke.

ITHACA KITTY

Caesar Grimalkin, a gray tiger cat with seven toes on each white front paw, lived with Celia and William Hazlitt Smith and their 2-year-old daughter at 116 Oak Avenue in Ithaca. William was an attorney and Celia was skilled in sewing and toy design. The Smiths had the cat photographed and had Celia's sister-in-law, Charity Smith, paint a likeness of the cat onto a three-piece pattern designed by Celia and patented the "toy animal figure" in October 1892.

The design was sold by the Smiths for one cent a yard to Arnold Print Works in Massachusetts, which then sold the printed pattern as "The Tabby Cat" on half a yard of muslin for ten cents each shortly before Christmas in 1892. Nearly 200,000 were sold nationwide that first holiday season. The sew-at-home toy made appearances at the 1893 Chicago World's Fair and in the windows of Wanamaker's department store in Philadelphia. Advertisements and articles appeared in newspapers and magazines around the world.

The Ithaca Kitty was especially known for its lifelike appearance and was allegedly used by farmers to scare away birds and by the Central Park police station to frighten away mice.

BOUNDARIES
OF IMAGINATION

Binghamton native Rodman Edward "Rod" Serling was one of the most prolific writers in American television, with over 200 teleplays developed during his 25-year career. He created, produced, hosted and (for the most part) wrote the half-hour anthology *The Twilight Zone*, aired on CBS from 1959 to 1964. A parachute infantry specialist during World War II, Serling was seriously wounded in combat, earning a Purple Heart. Resulting nightmares and flashbacks deeply affected the rest of his life and influenced much of his writing.

Each year from the mid-50s onward, he shuttled back and forth between Southern California and the Serling family home on Cayuga Lake (the inspiration for *Twilight Zone's* "Cayuga Productions"). Some of the most memorable scripts in television history were crafted in the office he had built in the backyard of the Sheldrake Point estate.

From 1970, until his death in 1975, he taught creative writing in the Department of Communication at Ithaca College, the permanent home of the Rod Serling Archives, an extensive collection of television scripts, film screenplays, stage play scripts, films, and unpublished works.

THE BUSIEST
MAN IN ITHACA

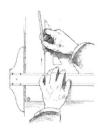

The first student in the architecture school at Cornell, William Henry Miller became Ithaca's most prolific and admired architect. Among the buildings he designed for Cornell were Andrew Dickson White House, Barnes Hall, Uris Library, Boardman Hall, Stimson Hall, Prudence Risley Hall, and the castle-like Delta Kappa Epsilon fraternity house. (On June 20, 1899, Governor Theodore Roosevelt planted two Norway Spruce trees on the west lawn of "Deke House" in memory of his fellow soldier and fraternity brother killed in the Spanish-American War).

In other Ithaca locations, Miller designed the Fiske-McGraw and Henry Sage mansions, the Elizabeth Van Cleef and Robert H. Treman estates, Greystone Manor (see **Exploits of Irene**, page 97) Ithaca High School (now the DeWitt Building), Greek Orthodox, Congregational, and Unitarian Churches, as well as the First Baptist Church, called the "Jewel of DeWitt Park" (financed by John D. Rockefeller).

Outside of Ithaca, he found time the Main Building at Wells College, Southworth Library in Dryden, and a private home for Supreme Court Justice Henry B. Brown near the White House in Washington.

SAVED FROM THE WRECKING BALL

During the remaking of downtown during 1960s "urban renewal," the City of Ithaca demolished such landmarks as the City Hall, the Public Library, and the Ithaca Hotel, but when it looked like the Clinton House might be next, a group was formed to protect other architectural treasures. Rescued by Historic Ithaca, the Clinton House now provides classrooms for New Roots Charter School.

Completed in 1830 as a 150-room hotel, Clinton House, with its massive Greek Revival-style columns, was designed by Ira Tillotson, a local architect and surveyor, and named for New York Governor DeWitt Clinton, the force behind building the Erie Canal, connecting Ithaca to the Hudson River – a promise of local prosperity.

William Henry Seward, Lincoln's Secretary of State, and Horace Greeley, editor of the *New York Tribune*, stayed in its rooms, as well as a number of actors from Ithaca's brief heyday as a center for the film industry (see **Cliff-hangers**, page 7). Simeon DeWitt (see **Ithaca's Founding Father**, page 47), resided at the hotel for several years before his death in December 1834. The adjacent Clinton Hall was constructed in 1843 to provide retail outlets for patrons of the hotel (setback slightly so as not to detract from the prominence of the portico).

TALLER THAN NIAGARA

No matter where you are in Ithaca, you are never far from the sight and sound of falling water – there are more waterfalls within 10 miles of downtown than any other city in North America. Among the most notable are Buttermilk Falls, taking its name from the frothy white cascade, and Devil's Kitchen Falls, the 28-foot wide crest of Lucifer Falls, plunging 115 feet over the gorge at Upper Treman Park.

Taughannock Falls one of the tallest single-drop waterfalls in the Northeast. Its 215-foot vertical fall is 33 feet taller than Niagara Falls, plunging through a rock amphitheater whose walls reach nearly 400 feet. Its name (pronounced tuck-han'-uck) is derived from the Indian word "taghkanic," meaning "great falls in the woods."

A 600-acre estate, once owned by Philadelphian John Jones, from the falls stretching all the way down to the edge of Cayuga Lake, was deeded to New York State in the 1930s, creating Taughannock Falls State Park. The oval shape, which can still be seen on the lawn near the park entrance, was once the Jones family's private horseracing track.

CALIFORNIA DREAMING

Cornell trustee, William Sage funded the construction of Cornell's original football field on nine acres of land just north of Fall Creek. The field was named in honor of the undergraduate son of J.J. Hageman, who donated the grandstand, cinder course, and dressing rooms. Percy Field was inaugurated on October 19, 1889 by a football contest in which Cornell defeated Rochester by a score of 124 to 0.

In 1960, Ithaca High School was relocated from downtown to a new nine-building campus, at the site of the old Percy Field. The design, utilized by Chicago architects Perkins and Will, is called "California-style," with the mostly-interconnected, low-slung buildings surrounding a center quad. (Open spaces, according to architectural theory, encourage the free flow and exchange of ideas and knowledge). Some have praised the campus as being architecturally innovative, while others have criticized it as inefficient and inappropriate to Ithaca's climate, as students routinely walk outside between classes, either out of necessity or for a more direct route.

Experimental Farm

In 1851, William Jefferson "Jeb" Williams hired architect Sam Graham to design and build an 11-gabled mansion on his farm at Shady Corners, south on Route 13 at the intersection with Routes 34 and 96 (converted to a restaurant and operated for 3 decades as Turback's of Ithaca). Howard Edward "Ed" Babcock (see **Let Them Eat Cake**, page 62), the first professor of Farm Marketing at Cornell's College of Agriculture, purchased the home from Jeb's son Rit in 1921, and established "Sunnygables" as a testing ground for farming innovations and food nutrition standards. Today, every American dinner table experiences the changes effected by this farm.

A national leader in American agriculture, Babcock was a driving force behind the Grange League Federation (GLF), known today as Agway. Under his leadership, it became a model for cooperatives throughout the nation. During the Great Depression he put the Farm Credit Administration on a sound operating basis. Then, as president of the National Council of Farmer Cooperatives in 1941, he helped to mobilize the work of cooperatives to meet wartime agricultural needs.

THE GREAT BAILOUT
OF 1925

During a 1925 meeting at the Ithaca Hotel, attended by a number of the city's businessmen, J. DuPratt White spoke of the advantages of living in Ithaca and pointed out that "Cornell's location here makes the city a better place to live than other towns of the same size without such an institution." The purpose of the meeting was to raise local funds "for Cornell's general operating expenses and to refund the present deficit of the University."

A citizens' committee was formed, headed by former mayor Louis P. Smith and Jacob Rothschild, owner of the city's "Boston-style" department store. Businesses displayed posters bearing the campaign slogan, "Itha-Can Aid Cornell," a message carried in banners over the streets, advertising in the newspapers, and cards in the trolleys. Students in the city schools wrote essays on the contributions of Cornell to Ithaca, and a huge replica of the library tower was mounted on the corner of the Rothschild store on East State Street, with the dial of the clock marking the progress of money raised.

1,072 citizens of the home city contributed $42,781 to the university, nearly $8,000 more than the goal of $35,000.

POOR MAN'S PIZZA

Generations of Cornellians have satisfied late-night food cravings at two legendary food trucks, Louie's Lunch and the Hot Truck. Greek immigrant Louis "Louie" Zounakos started with a pushcart in 1918, eventually replaced with a Ford truck he parked across the street from Risley Hall, offering mostly cold subs and sandwiches. In the late 1940s, Louie bought a new truck, painted in Cornell colors of red and white, equipped with stainless steel counters and electrical facilities, custom-made in Cortland.

In 1960, the Hot Truck appeared on Stewart Avenue, manned by Bob Petrillose, whose family operated Johnny's Big Red Grill. Bob's claim to fame was an original combination of tomato sauce, mozzarella, and toppings on buttered French bread, dubbed the "Poor Man's Pizza," offered seven nights a week from 10 PM until as late as 5 AM.

When C. Alan MacDonald, a graduate of Cornell's School of Hotel Administration, became CEO of the Stouffer Food Corporation, one of the new products he introduced was inspired by his late night munchies at the Hot Truck. Stouffer's French Bread Pizza has become one of the frozen food division's most successful products.

 # JENNIE'S BELLS

Born in Dryden on September 14, 1840, Jennie McGraw was the daughter of merchant John McGraw who earned a fortune in lumber and land in Wisconsin, Michigan, and New York. She shared her father's interest in Ezra Cornell's dream, and she gave the university its set of chimes, cast at the Meneely and Company bell foundry in Watervliet, New York. Housed in 173-foot McGraw Tower, the chimes were first rung at the school's opening ceremony in 1868. Three years later, a Seth Thomas clock mechanism was installed, and a large bell was added to the chimes to ring the hours.

One of Cornell's most-beloved traditions, the chimes are played by student chimemasters, three or more 15-minute concerts a day during the school year with a reduced number of performances when classes are not in session. Morning concerts include the "Jennie McGraw Rag," a carillon classic, christened in honor of the donor. Midday concerts are concluded with the Cornell Alma Mater (see **Timeless Tune**, page 93). The final musical piece is the "Cornell Evening Song" (the traditional German tune of "O Tannenbaum").

ITHACA TO MARATHON MARATHON

The term "marathon" comes from the legend of Phidip-pides, a Greek messenger who was sent from the town of Marathon to Athens to announce that the Persians had been defeated in the Battle of Marathon. For 25 consecutive years (from 1970 to 1994), a group of local distance runners completed the 26 miles 385 yards from Ellis Hollow Road in Ithaca to the Village of Marathon, the standard distance for the marathon race.

The idea of running a marathon to Marathon was the romantic notion of Jim Hartshorne, professor of ornithology at Cornell and founder of the Finger Lakes Runners Club, but the route turned out to be one of the hilliest courses in the country. Through Slaterville Springs and over the Harford hill to Marathon has 1600 feet of vertical rise (compared to 600 feet in the Boston Marathon), with the steepest climb beginning at mile 23.

Surely one for the record books, Ithaca High School Phys-Ed instructor Bob Congdon entered and completed all 25 races, each held on the second Sunday in October when local weather is most unpredictable. Bob's fastest time was 2:44, and his slowest was 4:01.

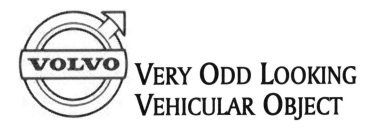

VERY ODD LOOKING VEHICULAR OBJECT

According to urban legend, Ithaca has the largest per capita inventory of serviceable Volvos of any city outside of Sweden, the local vehicle of choice for durability, reliability and longevity. With their super-warm heating systems, Volvos make great "winter rat" cars, needing only a good set of snow tires to navigate the local terrain. One can usually find an old Volvo in Ithaca inexpensively and drive it almost indefinitely. Since 1974, the Ithaca Foreign Car Service ("Dave and Dave") on West State Street has been in charge of keeping most of Ithaca's Volvos on the roads.

Every spring, the Ithaca Festival begins with a parade downtown, featuring floats, dancers in costume and other unusual displays, one of which is the Volvo Ballet, a celebration of the local automotive icon, conceived in the mid-1980s by the festival's music director, Heather Dunbar. Vintage Volvo cars and station wagons are adorned in makeshift tutus and, with Tchaikovsky's *Swan Lake* as accompaniment, they sway back and forth along the parade route like a flock of dowdy ballerinas.

THE LITTLE SCIENCE
PROJECT THAT GREW

Two volunteer teachers who began sharing the wonders of science with elementary students in the Ithaca School District planted the seeds for what is now the nationally renowned, community-built Ithaca Sciencenter, a museum that attracts 90,000 visitors every year. Before the old city waterworks was renovated in "community builds," Deborah Levin and Ilma Levine traveled from school to school with props and lab equipment giving hands-on science lessons. The Sciencenter's permanent home, designed by local architect Bob Leathers with over 2,200 Ithacans contributing more than 40,000 hours of work, opened to the public on May 22, 1993.

The Sciencenter's most notable achievement is the Carl Sagan Memorial Planet Walk, a series of 11 interactive stone monoliths, each one representing an item in the solar system, distanced throughout the city over the span of three quarters of a mile to an exact 1:5 billion scale of the solar system. The installation was created in memory of Professor Carl Sagan (see **Planet Ithaca**, page 32), a founding member of the museum's advisory board.

MOTHER OF ALL PRANKS

Cornell's McGraw Tower houses the oldest continuous-ly played set of chimes (see **Jennie's Bells**, page 88) on an American college campus, marking the hours and chiming concerts since the original set of bells first rang at the university's opening ceremonies on October 7, 1868. Almost exactly 129 years to that day, October 8, 1997, an astonishing, 60-pound pumpkin appeared atop the 173-foot tower, speared through the lightning rod at its apex, and remaining on the lofty perch for most of the following winter.

The mystery and sheer daring of the prank generated coverage by the national news media, beginning with an article in *The New York Times* on October 27. While there is a staircase leading to the tower's chimes, open to the public at specified times, and a small service hatch above the bells that opens to the bottom of the slanted roof, a prankster would have had to scale an additional 20 feet of the steeply pitched metal roof to reach the bottom of the lightning rod. No one has ever come forward with information about the identity of the perpetrator or the method of his madness. The pumpkin remained on the tower until it was removed with a crane on March 13, 1998.

TIMELESS TUNE

"Annie Lisle" is the name of a haunting ballad composed by Boston minstrel performer Henry S. Thompson, published in 1857, recounting the gradual decline and death of a young woman from tuberculosis, or "consumption," as it was called at the time. (Wave, willows; murmur, waters; Golden sunbeams, smile; Earthly music cannot waken Lovely Annie Lisle.) The song might have slipped into obscurity had it not been for Cornell roommates Archibald Croswell Weeks and Wilmot Moses Smith who in 1870 collaborated in rewriting six verses of lyrics that personify and revere the university.

"Far Above Cayuga's Waters" is considered to be one of the best-known alma maters in the world and many other colleges and high schools, almost certainly influenced by Cornell's version, have since created their own renditions. The solemn and hymn-like song traditionally concludes campus concerts by the Cornell University Glee Club and Chorus, and is played by the Big Red Band at Cornell sporting events. It is a parting song at the conclusion of graduation ceremonies, sung in unison with heads uncovered.

FORBIDDEN LOVE

With its beautiful setting along Fall Creek, charming architecture, and two single-lane bridges, you would never guess that Forest Home was the setting for what the *Ithaca Journal* called "one of the most extraordinary and heart-rending tragedies it has ever become our duty to report."

An early creekside sawmill in the hamlet, at the time called Free Hollow, was home to a number of woodworkers, and one particular cabinet shop, operated by local undertaker, William Criddle, also built coffins. When Montgomery Cornell, the 19-year-old nephew of Ezra Cornell, fell in love with Lucy Criddle, the undertaker's daughter, his family opposed any thoughts of "marrying out" of a family of "birthright" Quakers. On the Sunday morning of June 16, 1861, Lucy was found shot dead in Montgomery's buggy, and Montgomery was discovered drowned in the gorge behind The Byway in a double suicide that sent all of Ithaca into a state of shock.

Ever since that tragic event in Forest Home, the footpath along the bank of Fall Creek, opposite The Byway, has been called "Lover's Walk."

ITHACA JOURNAL-ISM

Older than even *The New York Times*, the *Ithaca Journal* traces its origin to publisher Jonathan Ingersoll and his *Seneca Republican*, its first issue printed on Independence Day, 1815. A year later, the paper was snapped up by Ebenezer Mack, who in 1823 decided the hometown paper should be called the *Ithaca Journal*. Bought and sold several times during its early years, the weekly newspaper became a daily in 1872. When the *Journal* was purchased by Frank Gannett (see **American Newsboy**, page 43) in 1912, it was only the second local newspaper in what would become the Gannett media conglomerate.

Throughout most of its history, the *Journal* has taken puzzling stands on civil rights, labor unions, and women's equality. In 1887, the idea of votes for women was called "ridiculous," and a local parade of Ku Klux Klan was described as "an attractive spectacle." The newspaper strongly supported the Vietnam War, headlining a 1967 editorial, "U.S. Troops Must Stay in Vietnam." In recent years, the editorial page has more closely reflected Ithaca's left-liberal political climate, endorsing Democratic Party candidates and supporting progressive issues.

GOLDEN AGE OF PADDLEBOATS

Barely a dozen years after Robert Fulton launched the first steam-powered boat on the Hudson River, Cayuga Steamboat Company built a 120-ton, 80-foot-long, 30-foot-wide paddle-driven steamer "to ply from one end to the other of Cayuga Lake." Its 24-horsepower engine was built in Jersey City and brought to Ithaca overland by horse-drawn wagon.

The steamboat *Enterprise*, launched on May 4, 1820, was soon transporting goods and passengers on daily round trips along the west side of the lake. Early morning runs carried milk and ice from Ithaca to nearby cottages, and brought businessmen into Ithaca on its return. During later runs, the boat, loaded with groceries and supplies, took passengers down the lake for the day and into Ithaca for shopping. At 5 o'clock, it took shoppers and the businessmen home for the night.

As the commercial steamboat industry thrived on Cayuga Lake, new "sidewheelers" were built, many financed by entrepreneur Edwin Barber Morgan of Aurora, the first president of Wells Fargo & Company and founder of American Express. By the 1870s, competition from the railroads had put an end to the steamboat era.

EXPLOITS OF IRENE

As one-half of a dance team with husband Vernon, Irene Castle ushered ballroom dancing into vogue and bobbed hair (the "Castle Clip") into popular style. While Vernon was in the service, Irene arrived in Ithaca to star in *Patria*, a Wharton Brothers serial (see **Cliffhangers**, page 7). After Vernon was killed in an aviation accident, Irene met Robert Elias Treman of the Ithaca Tremans (see **Ithaca's Royal Family**, page 45), and the two were married in May, 1919.

After a honeymoon in Lake Placid, the Tremans gifted the newlyweds a huge stone house on Cayuga Heights Road (now the Sigma Chi fraternity). The Tremans had a Gatsbyesque time in a house filled with furniture from Wanamaker's, a swimming pool (only one in Ithaca) filled with salt water from Atlantic City, and a cellar was filled with the entire contents of a New York liquor store, closed by Prohibition.

Although a banker by profession, Robert turned producer and starred his new wife in four films, all financial failures. The storybook marriage ended in 1923 when Irene discovered that Robert had invested her own money in the movies, and that it had all gone down the drain.

WE'RE NOT IN KANSAS

When Ithaca Festival director Laurel Guy announced the event's 1995 theme, "There's No Place Like Home," she compared the arrival of spring in Ithaca to the scene in *The Wizard of Oz* in which the film changes from black and white to color. After living in a typically long winter of black and white, we get our first splash of color from the bright yellow flowers of forsythia bushes. It's a welcome sight, signaling the end of winter and heralding the beginning of spring, not unlike the breathtaking moment when Dorothy opens the door to Oz.

Named in honor of the British royal gardener, William Forsyth, cold-resistant forsythia bushes are one of the earliest spring bloomers, bursting into a fantastic display of yellow blossoms that spread from the ground to the tip of each branch, sometimes emerging when snow is still on the ground and no other shrubs are flowering. The blooms of forsythia are fixtures of the local landscape, often with rows of the bushes used to demarcate property boundaries, providing "living wall" privacy fences during summer and fall, after they have fully leafed out. Ithaca once held an official designation as "Forsythia City."

FEEL-GOOD CITY

Planet Earth's most recent ice age (20,000 years ago) was characterized by the advances of glaciers which ultimately covered much of North America — in Central New York up to one mile thick. They acted like giant bulldozers, sculpting a basin for what was to become Cayuga Lake, eventually filled in with water as the glaciers retreated and melted.

Ithaca's "hanging valleys" are routes of streams that plunge into the lake below, eroding deep gorges (see **"Ithaca is Gorges,"** page 4) into hillside siltstone and shale, transported downstream in tributary streams. Hard rocks resist erosion, while soft rocks are worn away. When a hard lip overhanging softer rocks breaks off and crashes downward, a waterfall is created.

It is believed that an abundance of negative ions plays a role in our physical and emotional health. The waterfalls that surround the city (see **Taller Than Niagara**, page 83) are natural generators of negative ions. When water falls on rock, it splits normally neutral particles into negatively-charged air molecules. Once breathed into our systems, they produce a biochemical reaction that increases levels of the stress-relieving, mood-enhancing chemical serotonin.

HAIL TO THE CHIEFS

President Ulysses S. Grant arrived in Ithaca by railroad on Sept. 28, 1876, met by local dignitaries and his son, Jesse Root Grant, a senior at Cornell. Over 4,000 people lined up to shake his hand at an Ithaca Hotel reception. James Garfield visited Ithaca in 1878, two years before he was elected President. Rutherford B. Hayes, then Governor of Ohio, came to Ithaca to enter one of his sons at Cornell. Grover Cleveland laid the cornerstone of Cornell's Memorial Chapel. Theodore Roosevelt paid several visits to Ithaca, once giving a campaign speech from the veranda of the Ithaca Hotel. William Howard Taft made three visits after he completed his one term as President. Franklin D. Roosevelt made a two-day visit to Ithaca in 1931 to attend the 24th annual Farm and Home Week of the State College of Agriculture. Yale first baseman George H.W. Bush played three baseball games at Cornell. In 1955, Ronald Reagan dedicated the GE building at Cornell's Research and Technology Park. As Vice President, Richard Nixon visited Ithaca in 1956. Harry Truman (in 1960) and Dwight D. Eisenhower (in 1963) lectured to overflow crowds in Cornell's Barton Hall. Gerald Ford delivered a lecture at Cornell's alumni reunion on June 11, 1983. Jimmy Carter campaigned in Ithaca during his run for the presidency in 1975. Bill Clinton spoke at Cornell's Senior Convocation on May 29, 2004.

WAR IS UN-ITHACAL

Quaker-born Ezra Cornell (see **Surplus Wealth**, page 8), a "curmudgeonly pacifist," might well approve of the anti-war sentiments that have taken hold in his city. During the 2008 Ithaca Festival, local peace activist Trevor Dougherty, a sophomore at Ithaca High School, organized 5,814 members of the Ithaca community (each with two fingers thrust into the air) into the formation of a giant human peace sign, establishing a mark for the *Guinness Book of World Records*.

Local anti-war activists have included Father Daniel Berrigan of the Cornell Catholic Community, who on September 9, 1980, with his brother Philip, and six others (the "Plowshares Eight") broke into the General Electric Nuclear Missile facility in King of Prussia, Pennsylvania, where they damaged nuclear warhead nose cones and poured blood onto documents and files. On St. Patrick's Day, 2003, Daniel Burns, Clare Grady, Teresa Grady, and Peter DeMott (the "St. Patrick's Four"), members of the Catholic Worker Movement in Ithaca, poured their own blood on the walls, posters, windows, and an American flag at the military recruiting center in Lansing to protest the imminent invasion of Iraq.

THOU SHALT NOT KILL

The local SPCA was incorporated in Ithaca on February 6, 1901, to prevent carriage horse abuse in the days before automobiles. In 1904, the organization acquired sheltering facilities and took over as pound master for some of the municipalities within the county. For much of its history, the local SPCA has provided sheltering for unwanted dogs and cats, often forced to humanely euthanize animals due to the large volume of homeless pets in the county.

The "No Kill" movement, launched in San Francisco in 1994, was embraced by the Tompkins County SPCA on June 11, 2001, and Ithaca transitioned over a two-year period to a No-Kill community (supported in the effort by Maddie's Fund, the pet rescue foundation funded by David Duffield, Cornell engineering school alumnus).

Ithaca was the first and, to date, remains the only "No Kill, Open Admission" companion animal shelter, never euthanizing healthy, treatable animals while never turning away strays or surrendered pets. *Animal People*, a prominent national journal on animal issues, ranked Ithaca the safest community for companion animals in the United States.

PEOPLE'S GROCERY

The emerging counterculture movement of the 1960s inspired a group of Ithacans who wanted access to health foods, organic foods, and local produce. A local buying group was formed in 1971 and came to be known as the Ithaca Real-Food Co-op. Every Saturday, a few folks would drive to the Syracuse wholesale market to buy goods not available in Ithaca and bring them back to be divided among members. Grains and other non-perishable goods were purchased in bulk quantities and stored between bi-weekly distributions.

By 1981, the Co-op, now called "GreenStar," was managed by Dennis Hayes, its first paid employee, who changed business practices from the theater of the absurd to the theater of food. When a new storefront was found on Farm and Cayuga Streets, Dennis masterminded a human chain intended to carry items from the old space at the end of Fifth Street to the new one; the 400 people who turned out on a cold March day transferred the entire inventory, hand to hand, for eight blocks. After a fire in 1992, GreenStar moved to its current space (formerly Super Duper and Payless supermarkets) in Ithaca's West End, where non-members are welcome as shoppers while members receive a two percent discount (more if they contribute labor).

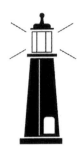

NEIGHBORHOOD BEACON

In March of 1927, the Francis Harper Women's Club, a group of Black women in the Ithaca community, organized the Serv-Us League to serve the residents of city's Southside neighborhood. With a mission to support the "uplift" of African-American citizens, educationally, spiritually, socially and economically, the group raised $220 for the Hope Chest as the seed money for what would become the Southside Community Center.

Through the efforts of members Vera Irvin and Gessie Cooper, local businesses were called upon to help, and an advisory board was formed. J.W. Hook served as the first president until his death when he was succeeded by Robert E. Treman (see **Ithaca's Royal Family**, page 45). For the first seven years of its existence, the Center met in a rented house at 221 South Plain Street, and in 1932, purchased the property at 305 South Plain Street, the current home of the Center. In 1936, the structure was razed, and in 1937 the current facility was construction as part of the WPA public-works program. The building was dedicated in a ceremony attended by then First Lady Eleanor Roosevelt in 1938.

Today, the Southside Community Center serves individuals of all ages, faiths, and ethnicities.

ITHACA ACCOLADES

The distinction of "America's Most Enlightened City" was bestowed on Ithaca in 1997 by *Utne Reader*, a magazine that calls itself a "digest of independent ideas and alternative culture." In 2001, Ithaca was listed among "Terrific Places to Bring Up a Family" by *Mothering Magazine*. In 2002, the city was featured in "Where to Buy a Retirement Home" by *Smart Money Magazine*, among "Top-10 Trips" by *Travel & Leisure*, "Best Places to Vacation" by *Money Magazine*, and "Best Mountain Biking Towns" by *Bike Magazine*.

In 2003, *Organic Style Magazine* called Ithaca the "Best Healthy City in the Northeast," and in 2004, *USA Today* named Ithaca among "Best Emerging Cities." In 2005, *Kiplinger's* listed Ithaca among "Great Places to Retire," then in 2006, as one of "America's Smartest Places to Live." Ithaca has since ranked among the "Hippest Hometowns for Vegetarians" by *VegNews*, "Best Green Places to Live" by *Country Home*, "Best Places to Live for Gays and Lesbians" by *The Advocate*, and "Best Towns in America" by *Outside Magazine*.

A 2010 poll by Gallup placed Ithaca at the top of the list of American cities for "overall well-being." Ithaca was ranked as "the most secure small town in the U.S." in the 2011 Farmers Insurance Group study.

 # GOODBYE YELLOW BRICKS

Practically everyone is familiar with the path that leads Dorothy and her companions to the land of Oz, however what some may not know is that the yellow brick road was inspired by a real street – in Ithaca.

The yellow-hued bricks originally used to pave a stretch of State Street were sourced from a brickworks which used clay with less iron than clay that produced more typical orange or red bricks.

As a young performer in a traveling theater troupe, Lyman Frank Baum arrived in Ithaca to court Maud Gage, a young woman from Fayetteville who attended Cornell. Legend has it that when Baum asked for directions to the university, and was told to "follow the yellow brick road." He traveled along those yellow bricks as he made his way up to East Hill, and in 1900 he immortalized the "yellow brick road" in his best-selling children's book, *The Wonderful Wizard of Oz*.

When they were torn up and replaced with more-common red bricks, the yellow bricks were re-used to build the solid brick house at 1114 East Shore Drive in 1939 (by coincidence, the very same year MGM's film version of *The Wizard of Oz* was released).

CAYUGA LAKE MONSTER

Just what might or might not be lurking in the shadowy depths of Cayuga Lake has captured local imaginations at least since January 5, 1897, thirty-six years before the Loch Ness Monster came to the world's attention.

On that day, an Ithacan, said to be a reputable citizen, saw what he believed to be a sea serpent with a large head and long body that disappeared beneath the whitecaps of the lake. (Other "cottagers" claimed that sightings of a creature they called "Old Greeny" actually date as far back as the early 1800s).

Then, in 1929, the term "monster" was applied for the first time to the creature by *The Ithaca Journal*, reporting the sightings of two, 12- to 15 foot-long serpentine, so-called sea monsters spotted in Cayuga Lake. In 1974, a teenager by the name of Steven Griffin was allegedly attacked by an eel-like creature while swimming in the lake. He emerged from the water with a broken arm.

Over the years, it's been speculated that the creatures might actually be descendants of some anomalous, aquatic animals that somehow survived extinction, perhaps trapped in the lake at a time when the ocean covered this part of the planet.

SHOEMAKER KICKS THE BUCKET

The first public execution in Tompkins County took place in Ithaca on February 3, 1832.

Local shoemaker Guy C. Clark brutally murdered his wife Fanny in a fit of rage after she had him arrested for domestic violence and serving ten days in the local jail as a consequence. At the trial, he said, "I swore I would kill her. I have killed her, and I am glad of it." The jury returned a verdict of guilty after 20 minutes of deliberation. His conviction resulted in a ghoulish public spectacle.

Clark was hung on an elevated bluff in Fall Creek on the cold winter morning of February 2, 1832, snow covering the ground. Thousands of spectators gathered to witness the event, some arriving on the previous day, and those who were unable to find accommodations camped out over night or found shelter in neighborhood barns and outhouses.

A band of music headed the procession which conducted Clark to meet his fate.

IT'S A SMALL WORLD

Charles Stratton was born a dwarf and at twenty-four years of age he stood only 32 inches tall and weighed 21 pounds. It was Phineas Taylor Barnum, the Prince of Showmen, who provided the stage name "General Tom Thumb" and hired him to be an "exhibit" at his American Museum on Broadway. Tom was introduced to a small woman who was also in Barnum's employ, Lavinia Warren, and the two were married in 1863. On their honeymoon trip, Tom and Lavinia were guests of President Lincoln at the White House.

In 1864, Barnum sent Tom on cross-country tour of America, accompanied by Lavinia, her miniature sister Minnie Warren (called the smallest woman in the world), and Commodore Nutt, another of Barnum's little people. On April 26, the troupe arrived in Ithaca for a well-attended reception at the Clinton House.

Much of the banter centered on Tom's fondness for attractive women, and he walked around the audience asking women for a kiss and selling his photograph and souvenir pamphlets.

 # SAFETY LAST

In the early part of the 20th century, "Daredevil" Johnny Reynolds toured the vaudeville circuit and traveled the country flirting with death as the "Human Fly," scaling the walls of tall buildings and balancing himself precariously over dizzying heights, aided only by his fingers and toes.

During a visit to Ithaca on July 23, 1919, Reynolds drew a crowd of 1,500 people to East State Street where he climbed the McCray building, "clutching only the spaces between the bricks." The crowd gasped as he grabbed a cornice and hung over the street to draw himself onto the rooftop. After reaching the top, he placed two chairs, one above the other, on a table whose legs teetered within an inch of the edge and balanced himself at the top, rocking back and forth as spectators held their breath.

Six local policemen kept the crowd in order.

TWAIN ON CAYUGA

"If you tell the truth, you don't have to remember anything," wrote Mark Twain, author of the classic American novels *The Adventures of Tom Sawyer* and *Adventures of Huckleberry Finn*. During the summer of 1876, it was Twain's 2-day visit to Ithaca from his summer home in Elmira that prompted an apology for one of his sins of omission.

As he explains in the preface to his short story, "Adam's Expulsion," he had visited Lake Seneca and promised to write a description of that visit for a woman friend. But he had "put it off so long that he forgot what the lake looked like."

When he wrote the introduction, he either forgot that the lake he visited was actually Cayuga, or changed the reference to neighboring Seneca Lake in order to disguise the location. The story was a forerunner of Twain's "Extracts from Adam's Diary."

NOTES

NOTES

NOTES

38560893R00074

Made in the USA
Middletown, DE
20 December 2016